THOR HEYERDAHL

THE
KON-TIKI EXPEDITION

Edited and abridged by
G. C

D1252982

Longman

LONGMAN GROUP UK LIMITED
*Longman House, Burnt Mill,
Harlow, Essex CM20 2JE, England
and Associated Companies throughout the world.*

*First published in this edition 1957
by arrangement with George Allen and Unwin Ltd.
Thirtieth impression 1990*

ISBN 0 582 53006 7

*Produced by Longman Group (FE) Ltd
Printed in Hong Kong*

THE BRIDGE SERIES

The *Bridge Series* is intended for students of English as a second or foreign language who have progressed beyond the elementary graded readers and the *Longman Simplified English Series* but are not yet sufficiently advanced to read works of literature in their original form.

The books in the *Bridge Series* are moderately simplified in vocabulary and often slightly reduced in length, but with little change in syntax. The purpose of the texts is to give practice in understanding fairly advanced sentence patterns and to help in the appreciation of English style. We hope that they will prove enjoyable to read for their own sake and that they will at the same time help students to reach the final objective of reading original works of literature in English with full understanding and appreciation.

Technical Note
The vocabulary of the *Simplified English Series* is the 2,000 words of the *General Service List* (*Interim Report on Vocabulary Selection*) and there is a degree of structure control. In the *Bridge Series* words outside the commonest 7,000 (in Thorndike and Lorge: *A Teacher's Handbook of 30,000 Words*, Columbia University, 1944) have usually been replaced by commoner and more generally useful words. Words used which are outside the first 3,000 of the list are explained in a glossary and are so distributed throughout the book that they do not occur at a greater density than 25 per running 1,000 words.

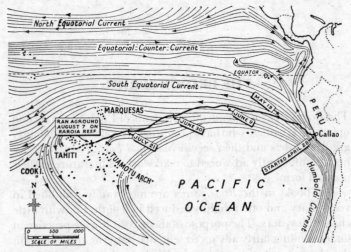

The Pacific Ocean

North Equatorial Current

Equatorial Counter Current

EQUATOR

South Equatorial Current

MARQUESAS

RAN AGROUND
AUGUST 7 ON
RAROIA REEF

TAHITI

COOK I.

TUAMOTU ARCH.

JULY 21

JUNE 30

JUNE 9

MAY 19

STARTED APRIL 28

Callao

PERU

Humboldt Current

PACIFIC OCEAN

N

0   500   1000
SCALE OF MILES

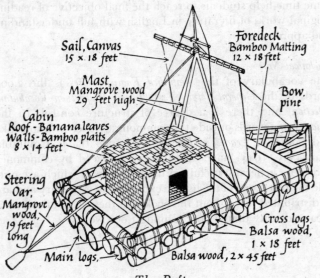

The Raft

Sail, Canvas
15 × 18 feet

Foredeck
Bamboo Matting
12 × 18 feet

Mast,
Mangrove wood
29 feet high

Bow,
pine

Cabin
Roof - Banana leaves
Walls - Bamboo plaits
8 × 14 feet

Steering
Oar,
Mangrove
wood,
19 feet
long

Cross logs,
Balsa wood,
1 × 18 feet

Main logs,

Balsa wood, 2 × 45 feet

Contents

Chapter 1

A theory

SOMETIMES you find yourself in a strange situation. You get into it gradually and in an ordinary way, but when you are in it you are astonished, and you ask yourself how it all happened.

If, for example, you go to sea on a wooden raft with a parrot and five companions, you will certainly wake up one morning on the sea and begin to think about it.

On one such morning I sat writing in a wet log-book:

" 17th May. Norwegian Independence Day. Rough sea. Fair wind. I am cook to-day and found 7 flying fish on deck, and some other sea creatures . . ."

Here the pencil stopped, and I began to think how it all began.

If I turned left, I saw a great blue sea with noisy waves rolling away to the horizon. If I turned right, I saw the inside of a shadowy cabin in which a man with a beard was lying and reading Goethe.[1] His bare feet were fixed in the roof.

"Bengt," I said, pushing away the green parrot, which

[1] Famous German poet (1749-1832)

1

wanted to stand on the log-book, "can you tell me why we are doing this?"

Bengt's book sank down under his beard.

"You know best yourself," he said. "It was your idea, but I think it's fine."

He moved his feet higher and went on reading Goethe. Outside the cabin three other men were working in the sun on the hot deck. They had brown skins and beards. Then Erik came creeping through the opening with his sextant and a lot of papers.

"98 degrees, 46 minutes west by 8 degrees, 2 minutes south—a good day's run!"

He took my pencil and drew a small circle on the chart which hung on the wall. This circle was the last of nineteen which stretched from the port of Callao on the coast of Peru. Herman, Knut and Torstein came eagerly in to see the new little circle that placed us forty sea miles nearer the South Sea islands than the last of the others.

"That means," said Herman proudly, "that we're 850 sea miles from the coast of Peru."

"And we have to go another 3,500 to reach the nearest islands," Knut added cautiously.

"And we're 15,000 feet above the bottom of the sea," said Torstein.

So now we all knew exactly where we were, and I could go on speculating why.

Perhaps the whole thing had begun the winter before in the office of a New York museum. Or perhaps it had already begun ten years earlier, on a little island in the Marquesas group in the middle of the Pacific Ocean. Perhaps we should land on the same island now, unless the

2

north-east wind sent us farther south, in the direction of Tahiti and the Tuamotu group. I could remember the little island clearly, with its rough, rust-red mountains, the green jungle on their slopes, and the thin palm trees that waited along the shore. The island was called Fatu-hiva, and there was no land between it and us now; yet it was thousands of sea miles away. I remembered the narrow Ouia valley where it opened out towards the sea. I remembered how we sat there on the lonely shore and looked out over this same endless sea, evening after evening. I was with my wife then, not among bearded men as now. We were collecting all kinds of living creatures, and other things left by a dead civilization.

I remember very well one particular evening. The civilized world seemed far away and unreal. We had lived on the island for nearly a year, the only white people there, in a hut which we had built for ourselves under the palm trees, and we ate what the tropical woods and the sea offered us.

We learnt much about the problems of the Pacific. In body and mind we often followed the first primitive men who had come to those islands from an unknown country, and who had ruled the islands until men of our own race came there.

On that particular evening we sat, as so often before, on the shore in the moonlight, with the sea in front of us. We were filled with the romance which surrounded us. We breathed the scent of the jungle and the salt sea, and heard the sound of the wind in the palm-tops. The great waves rolled in from the sea and rushed over the land until they were broken among the rocks. There was a roar among

3

the millions of stones, till all grew quiet again and the sea water drew back to gather strength for a new attack.

"It's strange," said my wife, "but there are never breakers like these on the other side of the island."

"No," I said. "But this is the windward side. There are always waves running in on this side."

We sat there and admired the sea, which always rolled in from eastward, eastward, eastward. It was the eternal east wind, the trade wind, which rolled the sea forward. Here the sea was stopped and broken by the rocks, while the east wind rose above the coast and woods and mountains, and continued to the west, from island to island, towards the sunset.

This had always happened, and the first men who reached these islands knew it. And we knew that 4,300 sea miles away lay the open coast of South America, and there was nothing but sea between.

We listened to an old man who sat, half-naked, before us and stared down into a little burnt-out fire.

"Tiki," said the old man quietly. "He was both god and chief. It was Tiki who brought my ancestors to these islands where we live now. Before that we lived in a big country beyond the sea."

The old man sat thinking. He remembered the ancient times, and he worshipped his ancestors and their deeds, back to the time of the gods. Old Tei Tetua was the only man left of the tribes on the east coast of Fatuhiva. He did not know how old he was, but his skin looked a hundred years old. He was one of the few men on these islands who still remembered and believed his father's and

4

grandfather's legendary stories of the great Polynesian chief and god, Tiki, son of the sun.

When we crept into bed that night, I remembered Tei Tetua's stories of Tiki, and the old home of the islanders over the sea. It all sounded like a voice from far-off times, which had something which it wanted to tell. I could not sleep. Suddenly I said to my wife:

"Have you noticed that the great stone figures of Tiki in the jungle are like the monoliths which are the remains of dead civilizations in South America?"

I felt sure that a roar of agreement came from the waves of the sea. And then they rolled back, and I slept.

Perhaps the whole thing began then. Certainly the events which brought the six of us and the parrot on to the raft began then.

When I came back from Fatuhiva, I began to study primitive peoples. The mysteries of the south seas attracted me strongly, and I wanted to find out who Tiki was.

Thousands of books and collections in museums in Europe and America offered plenty of material for use in the puzzle which I wanted to solve. But there has never been any agreement about the origin of these island people, and no one knows why this type is only found in the lonely islands of the Pacific.

The first Europeans who crossed the great Pacific were surprised to find these isolated islands. Where had their people come from? They spoke a language which no other people knew, and the newcomers found cultivated fields and villages with temples and huts on all the islands. On some islands they found old pyramids, good roads and stone statues as high as a house in Europe with four floors. But no one knew where the people had come from.

There have been many suggestions. Malaya, India, China, Japan, Arabia, Egypt, the Caucasus, Atlantis,[1] even Germany and Norway, have been suggested as the homeland of the Polynesians. But no answer has ever been decisive.

Some people noticed that the monoliths found on Easter Island were like those in South America. Perhaps there had once been a bridge of land over the sea, and perhaps this had sunk. But it has been proved from a study of the insects on the South Sea islands that in all the history of mankind these islands have never been joined with each other or with any other mass of land.

Therefore the original Polynesian race must have sailed to the islands, and this must have happened not many centuries ago; for they have not developed different languages in the different islands. It is thousands of sea miles from Hawaii to New Zealand, and from Samoa to Easter Island; yet all these tribes speak the Polynesian language. Writing was almost unknown on the islands, but they had schools where they learnt history and religion. They worshipped their dead chiefs, back to Tiki's time, and they said that Tiki himself was the son of the sun.

Men on almost every island could tell the names of all the island's chiefs back to the time when it was first peopled. Modern investigators have collected these names

---

[1] An island which is said to have existed in the ocean west of what is now called Gibraltar.

from the different islands and they have found that they agree together surprisingly; even the numbers of generations agree. By taking a Polynesian generation to be twenty-five years, it has been found that the South Sea islands were not peopled before about A.D. 500. Later some new men with their new chiefs reached the islands about A.D. 1100.

Where did these immigrants come from? Although they were intelligent, they were a Stone Age people; they brought stone tools with them. And in A.D. 500 or A.D. 1100 the only Stone Age people still in the world were in America. There even the highest Indian civilizations knew nothing of the use of iron.

These Indian civilizations were the Polynesians' nearest relations to the east. To westward there lived only the black-skinned people of Australia and Melanesia, and beyond them were Indonesia and Asia, where the Stone Age lay very far back in time.

Thus my attention in the search was turned away from the Old World towards America. The nearest coast to the east of the islands was Peru, which was full of indications if one looked for them. Here an unknown people had once built one of the world's strangest civilizations, and had then disappeared. They left behind them enormous stone statues and pyramids built in steps like those on Tahiti and Samoa. With stone axes they cut great blocks, moved them for miles, and set them up on end or placed them on top of one another to form gateways and walls, exactly as we find them on some of the islands of the Pacific.

When the Spaniards first came to Peru, the Inca Indians

told them that the enormous monuments in the country were put up by a race of white gods who had lived there before the Incas themselves. These gods were described as wise, peaceful instructors who had come from the north long before, and had taught the Incas architecture and agriculture. They had white skins and long beards, and were taller than the Incas. Finally they left Peru as suddenly as they had come, and they disappeared for ever across the Pacific to the west.

When the Europeans came to the Pacific islands they were astonished to find that many of the natives had beards and almost white skins. Sometimes the hair was reddish, the eyes blue-grey. But the other Polynesians had golden-brown skins and black hair. The red-haired men called themselves *urukehu* and said that they were directly descended from the first chiefs of the islands, who were white gods. Some of the people of Easter Island said that their ancestors came across the sea from a mountainous land in the east.

As I followed these signs, I found in Peru surprising indications which made me go on with greater interest to find the place of origin of the Polynesian god, Tiki. And I found what I wanted. I was reading the Inca stories of the sun-king Virakocha, who was the head of the vanished white people in Peru. I read:

"The original name of the sun-god Virakocha was Kon-Tiki, which means Sun-Tiki or Fire-Tiki. Kon-Tiki was the high priest and sun-king of the white men who left the enormous ruins on the shore of Lake Titicaca. These men were attacked and killed in a battle on an island in Lake Titicaca, but Kon-Tiki himself and his closest friends escaped and went to the Pacific coast; from there they finally disappeared over the sea to the west."

I was now sure that the chief-god Sun-Tiki of Peru was the same as the chief-god Tiki, son of the sun, whom the inhabitants of the Pacific islands claimed as the original founder of their race. But all over Polynesia I found signs that Kon-Tiki's peaceful race had not been able to hold the islands alone for long. Other men with a new civilization had come to the islands and mixed their blood with that of Kon-Tiki's race. This was the second Stone Age people that came to Polynesia about A.D. 1100.

But when I was looking for more signs, the war broke out and I joined the army. Peace came, and one day my new theory was complete. I had to go to America to tell others about it.

Chapter 2

An expedition is born

I SAT with an old man in a dark office in a big museum in New York. We were surrounded by things of the past, and by books, some of which the old man had written.

"No!" he said. "Never! You're wrong."

"But you haven't read my arguments yet," I said, pointing to the manuscript on the table.

"Arguments!" he said. "You can't solve racial problems by arguments."

"Why not?"

"The work of science is to find things out, not to prove this or that. It is quite true that South America was the home of the most curious civilizations of the past. But we know that none of the people of South America reached the islands of the Pacific. They couldn't get there. They had no boats!"

"They had rafts," I objected. "Balsa-wood rafts."

The old man smiled. "Well," he said, "you can try a trip from Peru to the Pacific islands on a balsa-wood raft."

I could find nothing to say. It was getting late. We both stood up. The old scientist took me to the door and said that if I wanted help, I had only to come to him. But

I must specialize on Polynesia *or* America, and not mix them up.

"You've forgotten this," he said, giving me my manuscript. I looked at the title: *Polynesia and America: a Study of Prehistoric Relations*. I put it under my arm and went out.

That evening I went to see an old friend, a thin little man who gave me some supper.

"No one will read my manuscript," I said.

"People think that you've got just a passing idea," he said. "And these specialists always work on one subject. It's not usual for one person to try to put together what is found in different subjects. What did your friend at the museum say to-day?"

"He wasn't interested either. He said that the Indians had only open rafts, and they couldn't have discovered the Pacific islands."

"Yes. That seems a practical objection to your theory."

"I'm so sure that the Indians crossed the Pacific on their rafts," I said, "that I'm willing to build a raft of that kind myself and cross the sea, just to prove that it's possible."

"You're mad!"

He thought that it was a joke, but I did not smile. I understood now that no one would accept my theory because of the enormous stretch of sea between Peru and Polynesia.

I had not much money at that time, and I went to stay at the Norwegian Sailors' Home where the prices were low. I had a small room, and I had my food with all the seamen. They were of different types, but they all talked of the sea and they knew it well. I learnt that waves and rough sea did not increase with the depth of the sea nor the distance from land. On the contrary, storms were often worse near the coast. A vessel which could sail near the coast could sail farther out, and small boats could dance freely over big waves into which a big ship would plunge. Most of the men knew little about rafts, but one of them had a great respect for them. "But you can't navigate them," he said. "They go with the wind, sideways and backwards and round."

In the library I found a description and some pictures of the Indians' big balsa-wood rafts. They had square sails and a long steering oar at the back. So they could be steered.

I sent copies of my theory to various cities, but no replies came. No one read them.

Then, one day, I bought a chart of the Pacific and went by train to Ossining, where I was often the guest of a young Norwegian married couple. He had been a sea captain and was now office manager for the Fred Olsen ships in New York.

After a swim we sat on the lawn in the hot sun, and I spread the chart and asked Wilhelm if he thought a raft could carry men alive from Peru to the South Sea islands.

He was surprised, but said yes. I was very glad and told him my plans. He said that it was madness to go.

"But you said just now that you thought it possible," I interrupted.

"Quite right," he answered. "But it may go wrong very easily. You have never been on a balsa raft. You may succeed, but you may not. The old Indians of Peru had generations of experience; when one raft got across, perhaps ten went to the bottom—or perhaps hundreds during the centuries. They had a lot of rafts together, and if one sank, the men could be picked up by another. But who's going to pick you up in mid-ocean? Even if you take a wireless, don't think that it will be easy to find a little raft on the sea, thousands of miles from land. In a storm you can be washed off the raft and drowned many times before anyone reaches you. You had better wait quietly here until someone has read your manuscript."

"I can't wait any longer now; I shall not have any money soon."

"Then you can stay with us. And how can you start an expedition without money?"

"People will be more interested in an expedition than in a manuscript."

"But what can you gain by it?"

"I can destroy one of the weightiest arguments against the theory."

"But if things go wrong?" he said.

"Then I shall prove nothing."

"You would ruin your theory, wouldn't you?"

"Perhaps. But one raft in every ten might have got across before us, as you say."

The next week-end I was back at Ossining again. When I left, there was a long pencil line from the coast of Peru to the Tuamotu Islands in the Pacific. My friend had lost hope of making me give up my idea, and we had discussed the raft's possible speed for hours.

"Ninety-seven days," said Wilhelm, "but that's in ideal

13

conditions, with a fair wind all the time. You must definitely allow at least four months for the trip, and you must be ready for more."

"All right," I said. "Let us allow four months, but do it in ninety-seven days."

I was much happier when I got home to the Sailors' Home that evening.

After some of my travels I had been elected a member of the Explorers Club in New York, and I now went inside. It was a rainy November evening. In the middle of the floor lay an inflated rubber raft and various other curious things. Colonel Haskin, of Air Material Command, was going to give a lecture and show a number of new military inventions which, he thought, would be useful to scientific expeditions.

After the lecture there was a discussion and Colonel Haskin said that active members of the club could, on their next expedition, take any of the new inventions if they let him know what they thought of them when they came back.

I was the last to leave the club that evening. I examined every part of all this new equipment which had fallen into my hands. It was exactly what I wanted. With it we could try to save our lives if our raft sank.

I was still thinking of it at breakfast at the Sailors' Home next morning, when a well-dressed and athletic-looking young man sat down beside me. He, too, was not a sea-man, but an engineer from Trondheim who was buying machinery in America. He liked the cooking at the Sailors' Home, but lived not far away.

He asked me what I was doing and I told him.

Four days later I met him again in the same dining-room.

"Have you decided whether you're going on your trip or not?" he asked.

"Yes," I said. "I'm going."

"When?"

"As soon as possible. If I wait much longer, the gales will begin. But I must get money first and organize the whole expedition."

"How many men will there be?"

"I've thought of six men. That will give some change of society on board the raft, and it is the right number for four hours' steering for each in twenty-four hours."

He stood for a moment, thinking. Then he said emphatically, "How I should like to be in it! I could do measurements and tests. Of course you must support your experiment with accurate measurements of winds and currents and waves. You're going to cross immense spaces of sea which are almost unknown; ships do not go there. An expedition like this can make interesting investigations; I could help you."

I knew nothing about this man except what an open face can say. It may say a good deal.

"All right," I said. "We'll go together."

His name was Herman Watzinger. A few days later I took him to the Explorers Club and we met Peter Freuchen, a big man with a beard. We showed him a map on the wall and told him our plan. He pulled his beard, and his eyes opened as wide as saucers as he listened.

He believed in the vessels of early peoples, and he had

himself travelled by raft down the great rivers of Siberia. As he told us about his travels, he said that we were going to have a fine time.

Because of Freuchen's eager support of our plan, things began to happen quickly, and the story got into the newspapers. I was called to the telephone on the next morning, and as a result of that conversation Herman and I, the same evening, went to a fashionable flat, where we were received by a well-dressed young man wearing a dressing-gown over a blue suit. He had a cold and held a scented handkerchief under his nose; but in the war he had been a famous airman. With him were two journalists, one of them well known.

Our host said that he was interested in our expedition, and would supply the necessary capital if we would write newspaper articles and give lectures after our return. We agreed, and our money troubles were over. Herman and I had then only to build the raft, get the men, and leave before the storms began.

Next day Herman resigned his post, and we started work seriously. Air Material Command had already promised to send everything that I had asked for, and more, through the Explorers Club. We must now find four suitable men to go with us on the raft, and obtain supplies for the journey.

The party of men who were going on the raft together had to be chosen with care; otherwise there would be quarrels after a month on the sea. I did not want sailors; they did not know much about managing a raft, and I did not want people to say afterwards, when we had succeeded, that it was because we were better sailors than the old raft-builders of Peru. But we needed one man who could use a sextant and mark our course on a chart.

"I know a painter," I said to Herman. "He's a big man and sailed round the world several times before he started to paint. He can navigate, and I've known him since we were boys. His name's Erik Hesselberg. I'll write and ask him. I'm sure he'll come."

"He sounds all right," Herman said. "And then we want someone who can manage the wireless."

"Wireless!" I cried. "We don't want a wireless on a prehistoric raft!"

"We do. It won't affect your theory unless we send a message for help. And we need it to send out weather reports."

"Then I shall write to Knut Haugland and Torstein Raaby," I said.

"Do you know them?"

"Yes. Knut was a wireless operator in the war. He was once surrounded by the Germans, but he fought his way out with his pistol. I met Torstein in Finmark. He had been hiding near the battleship *Tirpitz*[1] and he sent secret reports to England about it by wireless. He did other wireless work in the war too. I feel sure that both Knut and Torstein are tired of being at home now and would be glad to go for a little trip on a wooden raft."

"Write and ask them," said Herman.

So I wrote short letters to Erik, Knut and Torstein:

"I am going to cross the Pacific on a wooden raft to support a theory that the South Sea islands were peopled

---

[1] A German battleship which hid in Norwegian waters during the last Great War. It was later sunk by British aeroplanes.

from Peru. Will you come? I guarantee nothing but a free trip to Peru and the South Sea islands and back, and you will find good use for your technical abilities on the voyage. Reply at once."

Next day the following telegram arrived from Torstein: "Coming. Torstein."

The other two also accepted.

We had to find one more man, but there were difficulties. Meanwhile Herman and I began to think about supplies. We did not want to eat the same kind of food as the old Indians ate, but we were going to find out on the voyage whether they could have got fresh fish and rainwater while they were crossing the sea. For our own food I had thought of simple rations like those which we had as soldiers in the war.

Just at that time an old friend of mine, Björn Rörholt, had come to the Norwegian embassy in Washington. He was an energetic kind of man, and I wrote and asked him to find us someone in the American army who could deal with rations.

Two days later Björn telephoned from Washington and said that the American War Department would like to know all about our plans. Herman and I then took the first train to Washington, and we found Björn in his room.

"I think it will be all right," he said. "We'll be received at the War Department to-morrow if we take a proper letter from the colonel."

"The colonel" was Otto Munthe-Kaas, and he was quite ready to give us the letter. When we went for it on the next morning, he said it would be best if he came with us himself. We drove in the colonel's car to the Pentagon building, the largest in the world, where the offices of the War Department are. Our little raft seemed very small to Herman and me when we looked at the enormous building in which we were going to discuss it.

Members of the Kon-Tiki expedition (from left to right): Knut Haugland, Bengt Danielsson, the author, Erik Hesselberg, Torstein Raaby, Herman Watzinger.

Soon we were sitting at a large table with the head of the foreign section himself. This severe man at first could not understand what connection there was between the War Department and our wooden raft, but the colonel's careful explanation slowly brought him over to our side, and he read with interest a letter from the Air Material Command. Then he gave an order to his officers to help us in the proper way, wished us good luck, and marched out of the room. When the door was shut, a young captain whispered in my ear:

"I think you'll get what you want. It's a change from our daily work and it will be a good opportunity of testing equipment."

Herman and I were taken to see Colonel Lewis, a gigantic officer, who at once called in all the men in charge of experiments. Everyone was friendly, and we got more than we expected, from food to sleeping-bags. They took us to look at the things. We tasted special rations; we tested matches which lit even if they were dipped in water; we examined rubber bags and special boots, knives which would float, and all that an expedition could want.

The clerks made notes of the things and the quantities which we needed, and I thought the battle was won. But then the tall, friendly colonel suddenly said:

"Well, now we must go in and have a talk with the chief; it's he who'll decide whether we can give you these things."

We found that the chief was a little man with a very earnest manner. He sat behind his writing table and examined us with keen blue eyes as we came into the office. He asked us to sit down.

"What do these gentlemen want?" he asked Colonel Lewis sharply.

"Oh, a few little things," Lewis replied. He explained everything, and the chief listened patiently without moving a finger.

"And what can they give us in return?" he asked calmly.

"Well," said Lewis gently, "we hoped that perhaps the expedition would be able to write reports on the provisions and new equipment in the severe conditions in which they will use them."

The earnest officer behind the table leant back slowly with his eyes fixed on mine, and I felt myself sinking to the bottom of my chair. He said coolly:

"I don't understand at all how they can give us anything in return."

There was dead silence in the room.

"But," the chief suddenly added, and now a light had come into the corner of his eye, "courage is important too. Colonel Lewis, let them have what they want."

There are a thousand things to be done, mostly at the same time, when six men and a wooden raft and its cargo have to meet at a place on the coast of Peru. And we had only three months.

We flew to New York and Washington and got instruments and maps. We received a lot of good advice and some British equipment which was flown over from England to be tried on the expedition.

When time is short, and aeroplanes and cars are often used, money quickly disappears. We went to our friends in New York to ask for more money, and there we met some discouraging problems. One of our friends was ill in bed and the others could give us no money until he was better. We were asked to wait until he recovered; but we could not wait and it was too late to stop all our preparations now. So our friends agreed to leave us free to make any other financial arrangements we liked; and there we were in the street with our hands in our pockets and without money for our preparations.

"December, January, February," said Herman.

"And perhaps March," I said, "but then we must start."

Things looked bad, and for many days we could see no solution. But then Colonel Munthe-Kaas came into the story again.

"You're in trouble, boys," he said. "Here's a cheque to begin with. I can have it when you come back from the South Sea islands."

Several other people followed his example, and the private loan was soon big enough for us. It was now time to fly to South America and start building the raft.

The old Peruvian rafts were built of balsa wood, which, when dry, is lighter than cork. The balsa tree grows in Peru, but only beyond the mountains in the Andes range; so the seafarers in Inca times went along the coast to Ecuador, where they felled great balsa trees on the edge of the Pacific. We intended to do the same. But there are problems when one enters other countries with strange baggage.

"We must have an official introduction," said Herman.

One of our friends took us to the United Nations by car, and there we met representatives of Peru and Ecuador. Both promised to inform their governments. We also met Trygve Lie[1] and others, and I was given a letter to the President of Peru.

So we bought two tickets and flew to South America. We were worn out in the aeroplane, but we were relieved that the first stage of the programme was over, and that we were now going straight ahead to the adventure.

[1] At that time Secretary-General of the United Nations.

Chapter 3

To South America

WE crawled out of the aeroplane into a very hot day at Guayaquil in Ecuador, and were taken to the best hotel in the town. We had reached the country where the balsa tree grows, and we were to buy timber to build the raft.

In a few days we started trying to buy balsa, but we found that there were no big logs, which we wanted. The balsa trees on the coast had gone; they had been cut down in the war and taken away to make aircraft. We were told that the only place where large balsa trees grew was in the jungle in the interior of the country.

"Then we must go into the jungle and cut them down ourselves," we said.

"Impossible," said the authorities. "The rains have just begun, and the roads are covered with flood water and deep mud. If you want balsa wood, you must come back to Ecuador in six months; the rains will be over then and the roads will be dry."

In our trouble we went to see Don Gustavo von Buchwald, the balsa king of Ecuador. But he could not find us the logs which we wanted.

"A brother of mine has a big balsa plantation," said Don Gustavo. "His name is Don Federico and he lives

23

at Quivedo, a little town in the jungle. He can get you all you want after the rains, but it's no use now because of the rain in the jungle."

If Don Gustavo said a thing was useless, all the balsa men in Ecuador would say it was useless. So we had no wood for the raft, and no hope of getting any until several months later.

"Time's short," said Herman.

"And we must have balsa," said I. "The raft must be an exact copy of the old rafts, or we shall have no hope of coming through the voyage alive."

A map showed us that the jungle stretched unbroken from the Pacific to the Andes mountains. I had an idea. Clearly we could not go now from the coast through the jungle to the balsa trees at Quivedo. But we might reach the trees by coming down into the jungle from the snow mountains of the Andes. Here was a possibility, the only one we could find.

We got into an aeroplane with a man called Jorge, flew straight up the mountain side, and landed near Quito, the world's most peculiar capital.

Most of Quito's 150,000 inhabitants are pure or half-breed Indians. The city has some fine buildings and many low Indian houses, with narrow roads between the clay walls. These were crowded with mountain Indians in spotted coats and big hats. The air up here on the mountain was as clear as crystal.

Our friend Jorge found us an old hotel, and then tried to get us a car to carry us over the mountains and down into the jungle. But neither men nor car could be found to take us. The rains had begun and we might be attacked if we stuck in the mud. Only last year ten American engineers had been found killed by poisoned arrows; there were still many forest Indians who hunted in the jungle with poisoned arrows.

"Some of them are head-hunters," said Jorge in a hollow voice. "There are still people in this country who make a living by selling shrunken human heads to tourists."

Jorge did not know that Herman and I that same day had been offered two of these heads, those of a man and a woman.

"What would you say," continued Jorge, "if your friend disappeared and his head came into the market?"

As I went home I had a disagreeable feeling that Herman's head was much smaller than usual. But he had only pulled down his hat to protect himself from the cold night wind from the mountains.

Next day we saw a jeep from the American embassy and this gave us an idea. We went to the embassy and explained that we wanted some balsa wood which was standing in the Quivedo jungle, far below us. We asked for a jeep, and at a quarter past five the next morning a jeep arrived at the hotel entrance. An Ecuadorian captain of engineers jumped out and reported himself at our service. His orders were to drive us to Quivedo, whether there was mud or not. The jeep was full of petrol cans, for there were no petrol pumps on the way. Our new friend, Captain Agurto Alexis Alvarez, was armed with knives and fire-arms, because of reports of robbers. We got in and were driven quickly away along a good sand road southward through the mountains.

25

At a mountain village we turned off along a track which twisted to the west over hill and valley into the Andes. We came into a strange world. It was the mountain Indians' own world, outside time and space. On the whole drive we saw not a carriage or a wheel: only goats and families of Indians with their donkeys and mules.

We went up into mountains without a tree, and down into valleys of desert and cactus; then up to the snow and a biting wind. We reached the west wall, where the Andes range falls steeply to the lowlands and the track is cut along the edges of loose rock. We put all our trust in Agurto, our driver, and suddenly we saw the jungle far down, 12,000 feet below us. But then clouds rolled round us and we could see it no more.

Our road took us down, always down, and the air grew damper and warmer as it rose from the jungle below.

And then the rain began, at first gently. Before long it was beating upon the jeep, and the brown water was flowing down the rocks on every side of us. We almost flowed down, too, into a lusher world. When we reached the beginning of the jungle, the air was damp and warm with the smell of vegetation.

Darkness had fallen when we arrived at a cluster of huts, where we slept. On the next day we went on down through the jungle, down and down, though we thought we had reached bottom long ago. The mud grew worse but it did not stop us, and the robbers kept away.

We had at last to stop when the road was barred by a river of muddy water. We were quite unable to move up or down along the river bank. Some Indians near a hut told us that this was the river Palenque and that Quivedo was just on the other side. There was no bridge, and the water was swift and deep, but they were willing to take us and the jeep across on a raft.

The raft did not look strong, but it was twice the length and breadth of the jeep. Anxiously we drove out on the logs, and although most of them were under the water, they did support the jeep and us and four half-naked Indians who pushed us off with long poles.

"Balsa?" Herman and I asked, looking at the raft.

"Balsa," one of the men nodded.

The current carried us down the river, but the men steered the raft with their poles safely to the other side. This was our first meeting with the balsa tree and our first trip on a balsa raft. We left it and drove triumphantly into Quivedo. Two rows of wooden houses formed a kind of street and this was the whole place.

Don Federico's plantation lay a bit farther down the river, but he himself came to meet us. We gave him messages from Don Gustavo, and he welcomed us to his bungalow. He told us that he had known balsa rafts since he was a child. Fifty years ago, when he lived down by the sea, the Indians from Peru still used to sail along the coast on big balsa rafts and sell fish in Guayaquil. It would be hard now to find such big balsa trees as they had used; flood water and mud had made it impossible to reach the balsa plantation in the forest, even on horseback. But Don Federico would do his best; there might still be some single trees growing wild in the forest nearer the bungalow, and we did not need many.

Soon after sunrise Don Federico sent his men out on horseback to look for balsa trees which we could easily

27

reach. Don Federico took Herman and myself to a gigantic old tree which he knew. Before we touched it we gave it the name Ku, a Polynesian god of American origin.

It took a long time to cut Ku down, but late in the day he fell heavily into the surrounding forest. The Indians found and cut down other huge balsa trees, to which we also gave names. These were dragged down through the jungle to the river bank in front of the bungalow.

The logs, full of sap, were heavy; they certainly weighed a ton each. We rolled them out to the edge of the bank one by one and then into the river. There, held by ropes, they swung round and floated, about as much above as below the surface of the water. If we walked out along them, they remained steady. We bound them together with tough climbing plants from the jungle trees, so as to make two temporary rafts, one pulling the other. Then we loaded them with all the bamboos and lianas which we should need later, and Herman and I went on board with two other men.

We cut the ropes and went off down stream at a good speed. The brown men steered with big oars and easily kept the rafts in the swiftest part of the current.

Where the river Palenque joined the Rio Guayas, the water had risen so high that a steamer was sailing on it. To save time Herman and I got on board the steamer and sailed away to the coast, leaving our brown friends to follow with the rafts.

At Guayaquil Herman and I separated. He stayed at the mouth of the river to wait for the balsa logs; then he would take them on in a steamer to Peru, where he would

direct the building of the raft and make a faithful copy of the Indians' old vessels.

I myself flew to Lima, the capital of Peru. When I arrived, I went to the port of Callao to find a place where we could build the raft. But the whole harbour was full of ships, offices and so on. Curious people would pull the raft to pieces as soon as our backs were turned, if we built it there. There was only one thing to do. We must build it inside the walls of the naval harbour, where armed men stood on guard behind the iron gate. If we could work in there, we should be safe.

I went to see the Minister of Marine, and asked to be allowed to build a wooden raft in the naval harbour.

"Young man," said the Minister, "I'll be glad to help you, but the order must come from the Foreign Minister to me; I can't let foreigners into the naval harbour. Write a letter to the Foreign Minister, and good luck!"

I thought of the delay as letters went from one place to another and then disappeared.

The letter to the President, which I had, might be useful now, and so I asked to see His Excellency Don Jose Bustamante y Rivero, President of Peru. A day or two later I was told to be at the Palace at twelve o'clock.

The President's Palace is in the middle of the city and is strongly guarded by armed men. Soldiers took me upstairs and to the end of a long passage; here my name was taken and I was led through a great door into a room with long tables and chairs. A man dressed in white received me, asked me to sit down, and himself disappeared. A moment later I was taken through another door where an imposing man advanced towards me.

"The President!" I thought. But no. The man gave me a chair and disappeared. In one minute a servant took me through another door and I sat down, looking at a line of empty rooms whose doors stood open. A gentleman came forward and I jumped up. But no; this too was not the President. But I was told that the President sent me his greetings and would soon come.

Ten minutes later another man came in. I bowed deeply, and the man bowed still more deeply and led me through several rooms and up some stairs with thick carpets. Then he left me in a little room with one chair and one sofa. A little man in a white suit came in and I waited to see where he would take me. But this was the President.

He spoke no English and I no Spanish; so in a short time he left me and came back with the Air Minister, Reveredo, who could speak English well. Thus I was able to explain my theory to the President, who listened carefully and asked questions. At last he said:

"If it is possible that the Pacific islands were first discovered from Peru, Peru has an interest in this expedition. If we can do anything for you, tell us."

I asked for a place where we could build the raft inside the walls of the naval harbour, and for help from the naval workshops. The President nodded to show his agreement, and I was led out.

That day the Lima papers gave the news of the raft expedition, and at the same time announced that a Swedish-Finnish scientific expedition had finished its studies among the Indians near the Amazon. One of its members, Bengt Danielsson, was now going to study the mountain Indians in Peru and had just arrived in Lima.

I was writing to Herman in my hotel about the site where we could build the raft, when a tall, sunburnt man with a red beard entered the room. He came from the jungle, but his proper place was obviously the lecture room.

"Bengt Danielsson," I thought.

"Bengt Danielsson," he said.

"He has heard about the raft," I thought.

"I've just heard about the raft plans," he said.

"And now he wants to destroy my theory," I thought.

"And now I've come to ask if I may come with you on the raft," he said.

I knew nothing about the man except that he had just come out of the jungle and was a scientist. But he became the sixth member of the crew.

Soon six men were going to be packed together on a small raft surrounded by the endless Pacific. But just now the six men were separated. Herman was in Ecuador waiting for the logs. Knut Haugland and Torstein Raaby had just arrived in New York by air. Erik Hesselberg was on board a ship from Oslo. I myself was on the way to Washington by air, and Bengt was in a hotel at Lima ready to start, waiting to meet the others.

None of these men had ever met before, and they were all of entirely different types. So we should be on the raft for some weeks before we got tired of each other's stories. This was a good thing because the greatest danger before us was that a quarrel should start on the raft.

It was February when I came back from Washington. Knut and Torstein were busy preparing the wireless. There were a thousand things to do, and the piles of letters grew. Then one day a telegram came from Lima. Herman had been caught by a breaker and thrown on the shore, badly hurt. He was in Lima hospital.

One of the bones in Herman's neck was cracked; but his splendid condition saved his life and he was soon back, though blue and stiff, in the naval dockyard. There he had collected the balsa wood and started the work; and very soon we were all at the starting point.

The big balsa logs from the Quivedo forest lay there with yellow bamboos and banana leaves, surrounded by warships. The work on the raft was done with axes and long knives; naval officers, dressed in blue and gold, walked over and stared with astonishment at these strangers and their vegetable materials which had suddenly appeared among them. For the first time for hundreds of years, a balsa raft was being built in Callao Bay.

Nine of the thickest logs were chosen to form the raft. Deep grooves were cut in the wood to prevent the ropes which were to hold the raft together from slipping. Not a nail or a wire rope was used in the whole construction. The nine logs were laid loose side by side in the water, so that they might all fall freely into their natural floating position before they were fastened together. The longest, forty-five feet long, was laid in the middle and stuck out a long way at both ends. Shorter and shorter logs were laid on both sides of this, so that the sides of the raft were thirty feet long and the bow stuck out like a plough. At the back the three middle logs were a little longer than the others, and supported a block of balsa wood which held the wooden pins for the steering oar.

When the nine balsa logs were fastened together with the ropes, the thin logs were fixed across them on top about three feet apart. The raft itself was now complete.

A deck of bamboo was fixed upon it and covered with loose bamboo mats. In the middle of the raft, but nearer the back, we made a small open cabin of bamboo; its roof was made of leaves. In front of the cabin we put two masts made of very hard wood and fastened together at the top. The big square sail was supported by these.

At places where there were large spaces between the logs we pushed down five planks which stood on their edges down in the water under the raft. Centreboards of this kind were used on all the balsa rafts of Inca times, and they were intended to prevent the rafts from moving sideways with wind and sea. Our raft was a faithful copy of the old vessels in Peru and Ecuador.

We could now arrange the details on board as we liked. The bamboo deck did not cover the whole raft; we used variety to make us forget our narrow space. At the top of the mast we made a platform from which we could look at the sea from a different angle.

The Minister of Marine came to see the raft and was shocked by what he saw. I had to sign a paper freeing him and his department from all responsibility, and I had to agree that if I left the harbour with my men, it was at my own risk.

A few days afterwards I was sent for by the ambassador of one of the Great Powers. "Your mother and father will be very sad when they hear of your death," he said in a hollow voice. He begged me to give up the voyage while there was still time. A naval officer who had

examined the raft had told him that we should never get across alive. The raft was too small; it would sink in a rough sea and the logs would break. A big dealer in balsa wood had also told him that the balsa logs would float only a quarter of the distance across the sea and then the sea water would get into the wood and the raft would sink under us.

This sounded bad, but we did not change our plans. We received little encouragement from anyone. Storms would destroy the raft. We should always be wet through with salt water which would take the skin off our legs. Everything was wrong. A Norwegian captain told us that, even if we did not sink, the sail would not help us and we would take a year or two to cover the distance. One of his sailors said that we need not worry about that: in two weeks all the ropes would be broken, for at sea the big logs would continually move up and down and rub against each other.

If one of these arguments was right, we had not a chance. I felt anxious, but I had one comfort. I knew that a pre-historic civilization had been spread from Peru across to the islands at a time when rafts like ours were the only vessels on that coast. I thought that if balsa logs had floated for Kon-Tiki in A.D. 500, they would do the same for us now. My friends were not worried; but one evening Torstein asked if I was sure the ocean currents went the right way.

A few days before we sailed, we put food and water on the raft and all our equipment. We took enough rations for six men for four months. They were in boxes, and Herman boiled asphalt and poured it round each separate box to protect it. Then we put sand on them to prevent them from sticking together and placed them under the bamboo deck. We filled fifty-six small water cans with 250 gallons of drinking water. On the bamboo deck we fixed the rest of the equipment and some baskets of fruit.

Knut and Torstein took one corner of the cabin for their wireless. We had boxes of scientific instruments and films, and each man had one box in which he could put what he liked. Bengt took seventy-three books in his. We were ready to start.

First the raft was towed round the harbour for a time to see if everything was loaded well. Then she was towed to the Callao Yacht Club, where guests were to be present at the naming of the raft the day before we sailed.

On April 27th the Norwegian flag was hoisted, and also the flags of foreign countries which had supported the expedition. Many people of different races came to see the ceremony, and among them were ambassadors. One thing was quite clear to us: if the raft broke to pieces outside the bay, we would sail to Polynesia, each of us on a log, rather than come back again.

The raft was named the *Kon-Tiki*; a coconut was broken against the side so well that milk and pieces of nut flew into the hair of all those who stood respectfully near.

The sail was now hauled up, with Kon-Tiki's bearded head, painted in red by Erik, in its centre. It was a faithful copy of the sun-king's head cut in red stone on a statue in the ruined city of Tiahuanaco.

Before we sailed we said good-bye to the President, and then we went into the mountains to look for the last time at the rocks before we set out over the endless ocean. We went up to 12,000 feet and looked at mountain tops and grass. We tried to convince ourselves that we were tired of stone and solid earth, and wanted to sail out and learn to know the sea.

Chapter 4

Across the Pacific: I

THE Minister of Marine had ordered a tug to tow us out of the bay, and a crowd of people was waiting to watch in the morning of April 28th.

We six had little things to do at the eleventh hour, and when I arrived only Herman was there, guarding the raft. I got out of the car and walked the last part of the journey to stretch my legs for the last time. I jumped on board the raft among the fruit baskets and other things which had been thrown on board at the last moment. In the middle sat Herman, holding a cage with a green parrot in it, a present from a friend in Peru.

"Take care of the parrot a minute," said Herman. "I must go and get a last drink. The tug won't be here for hours."

As soon as he had disappeared, the tug arrived and sent a large motor-boat to tow us away from the other boats. She was full of sailors and cinema photographers, and soon a strong rope was fastened to the raft's bow.

"It's too early!" I shouted in despair. "We must wait for the others." I pointed towards the city.

But no one understood. The officers only smiled politely. The motor-boat started and the *Kon-Tiki* began her long voyage. My only companion was the parrot. People cheered and waved, and the cinema photographers almost jumped into the sea in their eagerness to catch every detail of the start of the expedition. In despair I looked for my lost companions, but none came. When we reached the tug I went on board and was so angry that the start was postponed and a boat was sent back to the land. It returned full of pretty girls, but without one of the *Kon-Tiki's* men. While the girls walked about the raft, the boat went back again for the lost travellers.

Meanwhile Erik and Bengt sauntered to the quay, but the raft had gone. There they met the rest of the party and saw the boat which was coming in. And so we were all six united.

The tug towed us out to sea; in the rough water all the small boats which were with us turned back, and only a few big yachts came out to the entrance to the bay.

The *Kon-Tiki* followed the tug like an angry goat, and pushed her head into the sea so that water rushed on board. This did not seem very promising; for this was a calm sea. In the middle of the bay the rope broke, and our end of it sank peacefully to the bottom while the tug steamed ahead. We were stung by jelly fish while we were fishing for the end of the rope, but we found it at last and the yachts persuaded the tug to come back for us.

"When a thing starts so badly," said Herman, "it must certainly end well. But I wish we had finished with the tug. This towing will shake the raft to bits."

We were towed all night. The yachts left us. In the morning clothes and logs and everything that we touched were wet with dew. The green water was surprisingly cold for twelve degrees south of the equator. This was the Humboldt Current, which brought its cold water from the Antarctic and took it north along the coast of Peru until it turned out across the sea just below the equator. All day long there was a wind from the shore here, but in the evening the wind blew towards the coast.

Erik, Bengt and myself got on the rubber raft and went on board the tug. The men showed us our exact position on the chart. We were fifty sea miles from land in a north-westerly direction from Callao, and we must carry lights for the first few nights so as not to be sunk by ships. Farther out there was not a single ship, because no vessels passed through that part of the Pacific.

We said good-bye; and many strange looks followed us as we went back to the *Kon-Tiki*. Then the tug left us, and we six men sat on boxes on the raft and watched the tug as long as we could see her.

"Good-bye, good-bye," said Torstein. "Now we must start the engine, boys!"

We laughed and felt the wind; but it was light and the sail hung loose.

We threw a piece of balsa wood on the sea at the bow, but the raft did not move past it.

"I hope we don't go backwards with the evening breeze," said Bengt. "I enjoyed saying good-bye at Callao, but I don't want to be welcomed back."

At last the bit of wood reached the stern of the raft, and we began to fasten down everything that had been thrown on board at the last moment. Bengt set up a Primus stove at the bottom of an empty box, and we were soon enjoying some hot cocoa.

"There's only one thing I don't like," said Erik, "and that's all the little-known cross-currents which can fling us on the rocks along the coast, if we get no wind."

But the wind came. It blew up from the south-east quietly and steadily. It filled the sail, and *Kon-Tiki's* painted head looked ready for battle. The raft began to move. The steering oar was put into the water, and we began to take our turns to watch. We threw balls of paper and chips on the water, and looked at our watches to count the seconds as the raft moved past them.

"One, two, three . . . eighteen, nineteen!" We were passing each of them in nineteen seconds.

Paper and chips soon lay in a line on the sea behind us as we went slowly forward. The *Kon-Tiki* did not hurry, but she pushed on with steady energy.

The steering arrangements were our greatest problem. The raft was built exactly as the Spaniards described it, but there was no one alive now who could teach us how to sail an Indian raft. We had to keep the wind behind us. If the raft turned her side too much to the wind, the sail swung round and hit things and men and the bamboo cabin, while the whole raft turned and went on, stern first. Steering was hard work. Three men fought the sail and three others rowed with the steering oar to keep the nose of the raft away from the wind.

The steering oar, nineteen feet long, rested between two wooden pins on a big block at the stern. It was the same oar which had steered the wood down the river Palenque in Ecuador. It was hard and strong, but so heavy that it would sink if it fell into the sea. It took all our strength to hold it when the seas struck it, and our fingers grew tired. Meanwhile the wind increased.

In the late afternoon the trade wind was blowing at full strength and it drove heavy seas against the stern. Now we fully realized for the first time that here was the sea itself, come to meet us. Everything depended now on the balsa raft's good qualities in the open sea. We could never turn back, because no wind would come to blow us back to the shore. Every day would carry us farther and farther out to sea. We must sail before the wind, with our bows towards the sunset.

We noticed with relief that the wooden raft rose over the first big waves which came towards us; but sometimes the steering oar was lifted out of its place or pushed to one side. Not even two men could hold it steady when the sea rose against us. At last we fixed ropes from the blade of the oar to each side of the raft, so that it could not turn much. We fixed it to the wooden pins with other ropes.

We were now in the swiftest part of the Humboldt Current. The mountains of Peru had vanished behind us. Darkness brought anxiety. We were not sure whether the sea was a friend or an enemy. When we heard the roar of a roller and saw its white top as high as the cabin roof, we held on tight and waited uneasily for the mass of water to crash down over us and the raft. But every time there was the same surprise and relief. The *Kon-Tiki* calmly rose over the water and then sank down again to wait for the next big sea. But when two big waves followed one another closely, the second broke on board astern, because the first was holding the bow in the air. The steersmen

43

therefore always had ropes round their waists so that they could not be washed into the sea.

We had fixed an old compass to a box, so that Erik could watch our course and find our position and speed. Two men at a time steered; they sometimes had to leave the oar while the masses of water thundered over them from the stern. Then they had to fling themselves at the oar again before the raft could turn. But every time the water ran easily back to the sea between the logs.

We saw the lights of two ships, but they did not see us. They were the last that we saw.

We became real sailors during those first days and nights. For the first twenty-four hours every man had two hours at the oar and three hours' rest. When a tired steersman left the oar he crept, half dazed, into the cabin and fell asleep at once in his salty clothes. But his three hours there passed very quickly, and he had to go out again to steer.

The next night was even worse; the seas grew higher instead of going down. Two hours together at the steering oar was too long; a man was not of much use in the second hour, and the seas beat us and flung us round and sideways, while the water poured on board. Then we changed to one hour at the oar and an hour and a half's rest. So the first sixty hours passed, in one continuous struggle against a chaos of waves. High waves and low waves, pointed waves and round waves, and waves on the top of other waves. Knut suffered the worst: he was badly seasick. The parrot sat angrily in its cage. The *Kon-Tiki* did not roll from side to side much, but we never knew which way she would lean next.

On the third night the waves were smaller, although the wind was still blowing hard. But about four o'clock an unexpected wave roared through the darkness and knocked the raft right round before the steersman knew what was happening. The sail tried to tear the cabin to pieces. We all had to go on deck and fasten everything and try to get the raft on her right course again. But she would not turn. She went stern first, and that was all. Two men nearly fell into the sea when the sail caught them in the dark.

After the sea had become calmer, we were so tired that we decided to wait. We took down the sail; and the *Kon-Tiki* lay sideways to the waves and rose over them like a cork. We all went into the cabin and slept.

We did not guess that we had struggled through the hardest steering of the voyage. Not till we were far out on the ocean did we discover the Incas' simple and ingenious way of steering a raft.

We did not wake till late in the day. Outside, the sea was still high, but not so wild as the day before. The sun was shining and everything looked friendly. What did it matter if the waves broke, so long as they left us in peace on the raft? She always rose over them. The old masters of Peru knew what they were doing when they used rafts instead of boats.

Erik took our position at noon and found that we had turned northward along the coast. We still lay in the Humboldt Current just 100 miles from land. The great question was whether we should get into the troublesome eddies south of the Galapagos Islands. If we did, we might be swept in all directions by strong ocean currents running towards the coast of Central America. But we thought that we should turn west across the sea with the main current before we got as far north as the Galapagos. The wind was still blowing straight from the south-east. We hoisted the sail, turned the stern to the sea and continued our steering.

Knut was now better and he and Torstein went up the masts where they experimented with wireless aerials. Suddenly one of them shouted from the cabin that he could hear the naval station at Lima calling us. They told us that the American ambassador's plane was on its way out from the coast to give us a last good-bye and to see what we looked like on the sea.

Soon afterwards we heard the wireless on the plane. We gave our position as exactly as we could, and sent signals for hours. The voice grew stronger and weaker as the plane circled round, near and far, and searched. But we never heard or saw it. It was not easy to find the raft low down in the troughs among the waves, and our view was limited. At last the aircraft had to return to the coast. It was the last time anyone tried to search for us.

The sea was rough in the days that followed, but the steering was easier. We noticed anxiously that the wind and the Humboldt Current were, day after day, sending us straight towards the currents round the Galapagos Islands. And we were going north-west at about 55-60 sea miles per day. The record was 71 sea miles.

"Is it all right on the Galapagos?" Knut asked one day. He looked at our chart where a line of circles (which showed our daily positions) pointed towards the accursed islands.

"No," I said. "One of the Incas is said to have sailed from Ecuador to the Galapagos just before the time of Columbus, but no one settled there because there was no water."

"Then we won't go there," said Knut. "At least, I hope we won't."

We were now so accustomed to the sea that we took no notice of it. We were always on top of the waves. But how long should we be on the top? It was easy to see that the balsa logs absorbed water. We could press water out of the wood with our fingers. Without saying anything, I broke off a piece of the wet wood and threw it into the sea. It sank quietly beneath the surface and disappeared. Later I saw two or three of the others doing exactly the same thing when they thought no one was looking.

But if we drove a knife into the timber, we saw joyfully that the wood was dry an inch or two below the surface. We calculated that if the water continued to be absorbed at the same pace, the raft would still be just floating when we expected to be approaching land.

In the daytime we thought little about the ropes, but when we crept into bed on the cabin floor, we had more time to think, feel and listen. And we thought of the ropes. As we lay there, we could feel the whole raft moving all the time. But the logs did not move together; as one rose, another fell. They did not move much, but we felt as if we were lying on the back of a breathing animal. After the first nights, the ropes swelled a little and held the nine logs better. But nothing was ever still, and the ropes took the whole pressure. All night we could hear them creaking as they were moved and rubbed. Every morning we examined them, and were even let down with our heads in the water over the edge of the raft to see if the ropes on the bottom were all right.

But the ropes did not break. The seamen had said that they would break in a fortnight. But so far we found no sign of wear. Not till we were far out at sea did we find the reason. The balsa wood was so soft that the ropes cut slowly into it and were protected.

After about a week the sea grew calmer and we noticed that it became blue instead of green. We began to go west-north-west instead of north-west, and we thought that we had perhaps got out of the coastal current and had some hope of being carried out to sea.

On the second day we sailed through a lot of small fish, and soon afterwards an eight-foot blue shark came along and rolled over near the raft's stern. It played around us for a time and then disappeared.

Next day we were visited by different fish, including dolphins, and when a big flying fish (see p. 130) fell on board we used it as bait and at once caught two large dolphins weighing from twenty to thirty-five pounds each. This was food for several days. We saw some fish which we did not recognize, and the nearer we came to the equator, the commoner flying fish became.

If we set the little lamp out at night, flying fish were attracted by the light, and often struck the cabin or fell helpless on deck. Then they had to lie there, for they could fly up only from the water. Sometimes a cold flying fish hit one of us in the face, but we did not mind; for they made good breakfasts. One morning we found twenty-six fat flying fish on the raft.

About four o'clock one morning Torstein was woken when the lamp fell over and something cold and wet touched his ears. "Flying fish," he thought, and felt for it in the darkness to throw it away. He caught hold of something long and wet which twisted like a snake, and he let go as if he had burned himself. When we lit the lamp Herman was sitting up with his hand on the neck of a long thin fish which twisted like an eel. It was over three feet long, with dull black eyes and a mouth full of long sharp teeth. Out of its mouth came another fish and soon afterwards another like it. These were obviously two deep-water fish which the snake fish had swallowed.

Bengt too was woken by the noise and we held the long fish under his nose. He sat up sleepily and said, "No, fish like that don't exist."

He was nearly right. We learnt later that we six were the first men to have seen this fish alive, though dead ones were known. Its name was the Gempylus. We caught another a week later.

Men usually cross the sea in ships with roaring engines, and they see very little of what is in the water. But on the raft we were level with the surface of the ocean. Every day we were visited by strange guests which twisted round us; and a few of them, such as dolphins, grew so familiar that they accompanied the raft across the sea and stayed around us day and night.

When night had fallen, the plankton around us were like burning coals. They were so bright that we drew in our legs when the shining little balls were washed round our feet at the raft's stern. On such nights we were sometimes afraid when two shining eyes suddenly rose out of the sea near the raft and looked at us. These were often big squids (see p. 130) which came up and floated on the surface with their devilish green eyes shining in the dark. But sometimes they were the eyes of deep-water fish which only came up at night, attracted by the light before them. Sometimes the raft was surrounded by heads two or three feet across, lying motionless and watching us.

We gradually grew accustomed to having these creatures under the floor, and yet we were just as surprised whenever anything new appeared. About two o'clock on a cloudy night the man at the helm saw a faint light down in the water which slowly took the shape of a large animal. Sometimes it was round, sometimes three-sided, and suddenly it split into two parts which swam about separately under the raft. Finally there were three of these shining things wandering round in slow circles under us. They were enormous; for the parts which we could see were thirty feet long, and we all gathered on deck and watched the dance below. It went on for hour after hour, following the course of the raft. The light on their backs showed that the beasts were bigger than elephants; but they were not whales, for they never came up to breathe. They took no notice of us at all if we held the light down on the surface of the water to attract them, so that we might see what kind of creatures they were. And, like all proper spirits, they had sunk into the depths when daylight came.

We never got a proper explanation of this visit, unless the solution was given by another visit which we received a day and a half later in the full midday sunshine. It was May 24th and we were moving slowly in exactly 95 degrees west by 7 degrees south. It was noon, and we had thrown into the sea the remains of two dolphins which we had caught early in the morning. I was having a swim when I saw a thick brown fish, six feet long, coming towards me through the clear water. I jumped up quickly on the raft and watched the fish, when I heard a call from Knut, who was sitting behind the cabin. He cried "Shark!" And as we were well accustomed to sharks, we knew that this must be something special.

Knut had been sitting there and when he looked up for a moment he was staring into the biggest and ugliest face any of us had ever seen. It was the head of a true sea-monster. The head was broad and flat, with two small eyes right at the sides. The mouth was four or five feet wide. Behind the head was an enormous body ending in a long thin tail. The monster was not any kind of whale. The body looked brown under the water, but both head and body were covered with small white spots. It swam quietly and lazily after us. In front of it swam other fish, and still others were firmly fixed to the enormous body and travelled with it through the water.

Using a dolphin as bait, we gradually attracted the monster nearer the raft. Its back rubbed against the heavy steering oar, which was thus easily lifted out of the water. We now had the opportunity of studying the creature closely, and I thought we had all gone mad. For we roared stupidly with laughter and shouted at the strange sight which we saw. Walt Disney himself could not have imagined anything more fearful.

The monster was a whale shark, the largest shark and the largest fish known in the world to-day. It is very rare and has an average length of fifty feet and probably weighs fifteen tons. It is said that the largest of them may be sixty-five feet long.

Again and again it circled under the raft, and all we could do was to wait and see what might happen. It followed us like a faithful dog, and the whole adventure seemed to us entirely unnatural.

In reality the monster circled round the raft for hardly an hour, but to us the visit seemed to last the whole day. It became too exciting for Erik and he thrust a harpoon with all his great strength down between his legs and into the whale shark's head.

A second or two passed before the creature understood what was happening. Then suddenly the stupid thing was changed into a mountain of steel muscles. The harpoon line rushed over the edge of the raft, and the creature stood on its head and plunged into the depths. The three men who were standing nearest were thrown down and two of them were burnt by the line as it rushed past. It broke at once, and a few seconds later part of the broken harpoon came to the surface two hundred yards away. We never saw anything more of the whale shark.

We were moving westward, just 400 sea miles south of the Galapagos. There was no longer any danger of our drifting into the Galapagos currents.

Chapter 5
Half-way

THE weeks passed. We saw no sign either of a ship or of
drifting remains to show that there were other people in
the world. The whole sea was ours.

It seemed that the fresh salt in the air and all the blue
purity that surrounded us had washed clean both body
and soul. To us on the raft the great problems of civilized
man appeared false and like a dream. Only the wind and
the sea mattered, and they accepted the raft as a natural
object. The wind and the waves pushed, the ocean current
under us pulled, straight towards our goal.

Bengt spent a lot of time with his books in the cabin,
and he was also responsible for the daily rations. Herman
was often busy with his scientific instruments. Knut and
Torstein were always doing something with their dry
batteries, and it was not easy for them to keep their little
wireless station working, a foot above the surface of the
water. Every night they sent out reports, and these were
picked up by wireless amateurs, who sent them to Washington and other places.

Erik usually mended sails and ropes, or drew pictures
of bearded men or odd fish. And at noon every day he
took the sextant and stood on a box to look at the sun

and find out how far we had moved since the day before. I myself had enough work with the log-book and reports, the collecting of plankton, fishing and filming. Every man had his responsibilities, and no one interfered with anyone else. All dirty work was divided equally. Every man had two hours each day and two hours each night at the steering oar, and duty as cook was regularly divided. There were few laws on board, except that the man on watch at night must have a rope round his waist. If an important decision had to be made, we held a meeting before anything was settled.

If there were no sharks near the raft, the day began with a quick plunge into the Pacific, followed by breakfast in the open air on the edge of the raft. The food was good, partly modern and partly belonging to Kon-Tiki and the fifth century. Our boxes of food were opened from time to time, and the asphalt outside each proved to be able to resist sea water. But tins were ruined by it.

Kon-Tiki had no asphalt or tins; yet he had no serious food problems. In those days, too, supplies consisted of what the men took with them from land and what they got for themselves on the voyage. They took dried meat and fish; and they carried water in skins and bamboos. They poured the water into the hollow bamboo and plugged the ends. A store of this kind could contain twice as much water as we ourselves used on the whole voyage.

We found that after two months our fresh water began to have a bad taste. But by that time one is through the first part of the ocean where there is little rain, and has long arrived in places where heavy rain can supply water. We did not always need to drink all our water ration. And every day fish were swimming round the raft and could easily be caught. To die of hunger was impossible.

One can quench thirst by pressing the liquid out of raw fish, and the old natives knew this trick, just as many ship-wrecked sailors knew it in the war. This liquid does not taste very good, but there is so little salt in it that it quenches thirst.

We needed less drinking water if we bathed regularly and lay down in the shady cabin. When a man is very thirsty in hot weather, he usually thinks that the body needs water. Yet it is not liquid that the body needs then, but salt. The special rations we had on board included salt tablets to be taken regularly on hot days, because sweat removes salt from the body. Sometimes we added sea water to the ration, and we found that our thirst was quenched, and that we were never ill afterwards.

The old Polynesians had some curious stories. They said that their forefathers, when they sailed across the sea, had with them the leaves of a certain plant. They chewed these, and their thirst disappeared. Another effect of the plant was that they could drink sea water without being sick. No such plants grew in the South Sea islands, and therefore they came from their homeland.

Modern scientists investigated this matter and reached the conclusion that the only known plant with such an effect is the coca plant, which grew only in Peru. For a fairly short time, the chewing of coca leaves will allow one to drink sea water without being ill, but we did not test them on the *Kon-Tiki*.

We had other plants in baskets, and they began to grow. It was like a little garden on the raft. When the first

57

Europeans came to the Pacific islands, they found large plantations of sweet potatoes on Easter Island and in Hawaii and New Zealand. The same potato was cultivated on other islands, but only in Polynesia. It was quite unknown in the part of the world which lay farther west. Many Polynesian stories centred round this plant, and it was said that Tiki himself brought it from his original homeland.

Now, as is known, America is the only place in the rest of the world where the potato grew before the time of the Europeans. The sweet potato which Tiki brought to the islands is exactly the same as that which the Indians have grown in Peru from the earliest times. The plant cannot bear sea water, and so it is useless to explain that it drifted across the 4,000 miles of sea from Peru to the islands. It must have been carried.

We had two hundred coconuts on board, and some of these began to grow. After ten weeks at sea we had a dozen baby palm trees a foot high. But the coconuts which were touched by sea water were ruined.

Crabs (see p. 131) often came on board the raft, where they ate any flying fish which the cook had missed. One of the crabs, which we called Johannes, was quite tame and lived by the steering block. We all fed him; he took bits of fish from our fingers and then ran back to his hole, where he sat in the doorway and chewed like a schoolboy, pushing the food into his mouth.

The crabs ate plankton washed on board by the waves. And these, the smallest creatures in the sea, were good eating even for us. They drift about with the currents in countless numbers, and are eaten by fish and birds.

Some are plants and some are fish eggs, floating loose. There may be thousands in a glass of water. More than once people have died of hunger on the sea because they have not found fish which they could catch. In such cases the dying men have often been sailing about in thin raw fish soup, and if they could have collected the plankton, they would not have died. We used to catch them with a special net. The smell was bad, but the taste was good enough. The uneatable vegetable plankton were either too small to be caught by the meshes of the net, or so large that we could pick them out with our fingers.

The whale, which is the largest animal in the world, lives on plankton. Great whales often rushed towards us, close to the side of the raft. One day something behind us blew hard like a swimming horse, and a big whale came up and stared at us. It was so unusual to hear real breathing in the water that we had a warm family feeling for our old distant cousin, the whale, who had wandered like us so far out to sea. I watched it with pleasure until it sank into the sea again and disappeared.

We were visited by whales many times. They passed us like ships on the horizon, or they steered straight towards us. We were prepared for a dangerous collision the first time a big whale approached the raft. We could hear its breathing as it grew nearer. We gathered on the edge of the raft to watch it, while one man sat at the top of the mast and shouted that he could see seven or eight more swimming towards us.

The big shining forehead of the first whale was not more than two yards from us when it sank beneath the surface of the water, and then the enormous blue-black back passed quietly under the raft. It lay there for a time, dark and still, and we held our breath. Then it disappeared from sight. Meanwhile the others had arrived, but they paid no attention to us. They quite enjoyed themselves among the waves in the sunshine, but about noon they all disappeared.

Most of the fish which followed us were dolphins or pilot fish. We did not know what drew them to the raft. Either there was a wonderful attraction in being able to swim in the shade with a moving roof above them, or they found food in the seaweed which hung from the logs and the steering oar under the water. This seaweed grew with astonishing speed, so that the *Kon-Tiki* looked like a bearded sea-god as she rolled along among the waves. We used to eat the seaweed sometimes, but it was not very good.

The dolphin was usually from 3 feet 3 inches to 4 feet 6 inches long, with flat sides and an enormously high head and neck. We caught one which was 4 feet 8 inches long, with a head 13½ inches high. The dolphin has a wonderful colour. In the water it shone blue and green, but if we caught one we sometimes saw a strange sight. As the fish died it gradually changed colour and became silver grey with black spots, and finally it all became silvery white. This lasted for four or five minutes, and then the old colours slowly reappeared. Even in the water the dolphin sometimes changed colour, and often we saw a copper-coloured fish which we found later to be our friend the dolphin.

When the dolphin was feeling pleased, it turned over on its flat side, swam at a great speed, and then jumped into the air and fell on the sea with a smack which splashed the water up at both sides. As soon as it was in the water again, it jumped a second time and then again. But when it was in a bad temper, it bit. One of them bit Torstein in the foot one day. After our return home we heard that dolphins attack and eat people when bathing, but we bathed among them every day.

The cook could always get a dolphin for dinner if he wished. The flesh was very good to eat if the fish was freshly caught. It did not go bad for two days, and that was all we needed, for there were fish enough in the sea.

We became acquainted with pilot fish (see p. 131) in another way. Sharks brought them and left them for us after the shark's death. We had not long been at sea before the first shark came, and they soon became almost daily visitors. Most of them followed behind the steering oar. The blue-grey body of the shark always looked brown in the sunlight just below the surface, and it moved up and down with the sea. If there were big waves, the shark might be lifted high above our own level, and then we had a direct view of the shark as in a glass case, while it swam importantly along with pilot fish in front of its jaws.

At first we respected sharks because of their reputation and alarming appearance, and our respect increased when we found that the ends of our hand harpoons were broken on the shark's hard back.

Once we fastened together a number of our largest fish-hooks and hid them inside the body of a whole dolphin. We threw this into the sea fastened to many steel lines. Slowly and surely a shark came up and swallowed the

61

whole dolphin. There was a struggle as the shark beat the water, but we pulled the big creature to the stern and over the low logs at the back.

Inside our first shark we found a lost harpoon head, and we thought at first that this was why the shark did not fight harder. But later we caught many other sharks in the same way, and it was always just as easy.

The pilot fish goes along with the shark, and when it acts independently it is only because it sees food itself. After a shark was caught the pilot fish swam about in a distracted manner, searching, and always came back and followed behind the raft. But as time passed and the shark did not return, the pilot fish had to look round for a new lord and master; and none was nearer than the *Kon-Tiki* herself. If we put our heads down into the water, we saw the raft as the body of a sea monster, with the steering oar as its tail. In the water the pilot fish swam side by side and took no notice of us. They were our pets and we did not hurt them.

We had been warned to be on our guard against the octopus (see p. 131), for it could get on board the raft. These creatures were so ready to eat anything, that if one was caught on a hook, another came and began to eat it. They had arms which could kill a big shark. We were told that they floated in the darkness, and that their arms were long enough to feel about in every small corner of the raft. We did not like the idea of cold arms round our necks when we were sleeping, and we kept sharp knives, one for each of us, in case we woke in the power of these arms.

For a long time we saw no sign of a squid, but one morning we found a baby octopus on board. A thick black

liquid lay on the bamboo deck round it. We wrote a page or two in the log-book in this ink, and then threw the baby into the sea.

One day we found a smaller squid on the cabin roof. This puzzled us very much. It could not have climbed up there, because the only ink marks were in a ring round it on the roof. It had not been dropped by a sea bird because there were no marks of a beak on its body. We thought that a big wave must have thrown it up there, but none of us could remember such a wave that night.

We found the explanation of this puzzle later. Young squids can pump sea water with great force through a closed tube along the side of the body, and can thus shoot backwards at a high speed through the sea. In this way they are able to escape from their pursuers; they steer up at an angle from the surface by unfolding pieces of skin like wings. Like flying fish, they make a glider flight over the waves for as far as their speed can carry them. This rapid movement frequently brought young squids on board the raft in the following months.

Squids can be eaten, but they do not taste very good. If we got any on deck, we exchanged them for something else by throwing out a hook with a squid on it and pulling it in again with a fish on the end.

We saw other strange creatures. The diary contains many descriptions like these:

11/5. To-day an enormous sea animal twice came up to the surface as we sat at supper on the edge of the raft. We have no idea what it was.

6/6. Herman saw a thick, dark-coloured fish with a broad white body, a thin tail, and spikes. It jumped out of the sea several times.

Next day. Erik was sitting at the masthead, 12 noon, when he saw thirty or forty long, thin, brown fish of the same kind as yesterday.

18/6. Knut noticed a thin creature, two or three feet long, which stood straight up and down in the water below the surface, and dived like a snake.

On several occasions we passed over a dark mass that lay under the surface, the size of the floor of a room. We supposed that it was the well-known great ray, of evil reputation. But it never moved and we never went close enough to see its shape clearly.

With such company in the water time never passed slowly. It was less pleasant when we had to dive into the sea ourselves and examine the ropes under the raft. One day one of the centreboards slipped down under the raft, where it was caught in the ropes. But we could not get hold of it.

Herman and Knut were the best divers. Twice Herman swam under the raft and lay there among dolphins and pilot fish, pulling at the board. He had just come up for the second time, and was sitting on the edge of the raft to breathe, when an eight-foot shark was noticed not more than ten feet from his legs. We pushed a harpoon into its skull, and after a struggle the shark disappeared, leaving a sheet of oil on the surface.

The centreboard was still out of its proper place, and so Knut suggested that we should make a diving basket.

After this was done we were let down in it beside the raft. Our legs were thus protected from sharks by the basket.

The light down in the water was wonderfully clear and gentle for us who were accustomed to the hot sun on deck. Even when we looked down into the bottomless depths of the sea, where the black night is eternal, it appeared to us a pleasant light blue because of the rays of the sun which came back from it.

There were not many fixed marks out here at sea. Waves and fish, sun and stars, came and went. There was not supposed to be land of any sort in the 4,300 sea miles that separated the South Sea islands from Peru. We were therefore greatly surprised when we were getting near 100 degrees west and discovered that a reef was marked on the Pacific chart ahead of us, almost on the course which we were following.

It was marked as a small circle and we found the following in a book called *Sailing Directions for South America*:

"Breakers were reported in 1906 and again in 1926 about 600 miles south-westward of the Galapagos Islands, in latitude 6 degrees, 42 minutes south, longitude 99 degrees, 43 minutes west. In 1927 a steamer passed one mile west of this position, but saw no sign of breakers, and in 1934 another passed one mile south and saw none. The motor-vessel *Cowrie*, in 1935, found no bottom in this position."

According to the charts the place was clearly still considered possibly dangerous for ships. But our raft was not a ship and did not need deep water. So we turned the raft and steered straight for the place to see what we found there. We were glad to see that the *Kon-Tiki* could be steered surely and steadily at an angle to the wind. For two days and nights we drove the raft north-north-west. The waves were high and they changed as the wind changed. But we were lifted up over all of them, though their tops sometimes reached six feet above the level of the cabin roof. We had a wet rest at night; water came into the cabin, rushing in over the provisions and ourselves.

We saw many fish on the next day, and some frigate birds that are usually considered as a sign that land is near.

" Perhaps there really is a reef," some of us thought. "Suppose we find a little green grassy island! One can never know when so few people have been here before. Then we'll have discovered a new land—Kon-Tiki Island! "

From noon onwards Erik often climbed up on the box and stood looking through his sextant. At 6.20 in the evening he reported our position as latitude 6 degrees, 42 minutes south, longitude 99 degrees, 42 minutes west. We were one sea mile east of the reef marked on the chart. We took the sail down; the wind was blowing from the east and would take us slowly right to the place.

When the sun went down into the sea, the moon shone out in all its brightness and lit up the surface of the water. We saw breaking seas everywhere, in long rows, but there was nothing to show a proper reef. As we drifted over the centre of the marked area, we measured the depth all the time. We had a line more than 500 fathoms long, and even if it did not hang straight down, it must have reached a depth of 400 fathoms. And we found no bottom, either east of the place, or in the middle of it, or west of it. We took one last look over the sea, and when we could safely say that there were no shallows there, we put up the sail again and laid the oar in its usual place. And so we went on with the raft on her natural free course. We could now sleep and eat dry.

On this little sailing trip to the spurious reef, we had learnt quite a lot about the usefulness of the centreboards. Later in the voyage Herman and Knut dived under the raft together and brought up the fifth centreboard. Then we learned still more about these curious pieces of board, something which no one had understood since the Indians gave up this forgotten sport. The board did the work of a keel and allowed the raft to move at an angle to the wind: that was quite clear. But the old Spaniards declared that the Indians "steered" their balsa rafts on the sea with "certain centreboards which they pushed down into the spaces between the logs" and this seemed incomprehensible both to us and to all who had considered the problem.

We discovered the secret in the following manner. The wind was steady and the sea had gone down again, so that the *Kon-Tiki* had kept a steady course for two days without the use of the oar. We pushed the fifth centreboard down into a space near the stern, and at once the *Kon-Tiki* changed her course several degrees from west towards the north-west, and went on steadily on her new course. If we pulled the centreboard up again, the raft swung back on to her earlier course. But if we pulled it only half-way up, the raft swung only half-way back to her old course. By simply raising and lowering the centreboard, we could change the course without using the oar. This was the Incas' ingenious system.

The centreboards which are nearest to the mast have the least effect in changing the course, and if the wind was exactly from the stern, the centreboards had no effect, and it was impossible to keep the raft steady without the oar.

We could certainly have continued our voyage by making the steersman pull a centreboard up or push it down in a chink, instead of moving the oar; but we had now become so accustomed to the use of the oar that we preferred to continue with it.

It was the forty-fifth day at sea; we had advanced from the 78th degree of longitude to the 108th, and were exactly half-way to the first islands ahead. There were over 2,000 sea miles between us and South America in the east, and it was the same distance to Polynesia in the west. The nearest land in any direction was the Galapagos Islands to the east-north-east, and Easter Island due south, both more than 500 sea miles away. We had not seen a ship and we never did see one, because we were far away from the courses of all ordinary ships in the Pacific.

But we did not really feel these enormous distances; our own floating world remained always the same, a circle of sea with the raft in its centre, while the same stars rolled over us night after night.

WHEN the sea was not too rough, we were often out in the little dinghy taking photographs. I shall not forget the first time. Two men sailed away from the raft and then they sat roaring with laughter. The waves lifted them up and down and their laughs rang out across the empty Pacific. We looked round us with mixed feelings, and saw nothing comic except our own hairy faces. But the two men in the dinghy must be accustomed to those, and we began to think that they had gone mad. They could hardly get back to the *Kon-Tiki* because they were laughing so much. With eyes full of tears they begged us to go and see for ourselves.

Two of us jumped into the dancing rubber dinghy, and were caught by a sea which lifted us away. Immediately we sat down and roared with laughter. The two who had not yet gone to look thought we had all gone mad, and we had to return to calm them.

It was ourselves and our proud vessel which made such a completely hopeless, mad impression on us the first time we saw the whole thing from a distance. We had never before seen ourselves from outside on the open sea. The logs disappeared behind the smallest waves; and when we saw anything at all, it was the low cabin with the wide doorway and the roof of leaves rising from the sea. And the raft was full of sunburnt, bearded ruffians. If a high sea rushed past, cabin and sail and the whole mast might disappear behind the mountain of water, but the cabin and its ruffians would certainly be there again the next moment.

It looked bad, and we could not realize that things had gone so well on board the peculiar raft.

Next time we rowed out to laugh at ourselves we nearly had a disaster. The wind and the sea were higher than we supposed, and the Kon-Tiki was moving fast. We in the dinghy had to row very hard out on the open sea in an attempt to reach the unmanageable raft, which could not stop or wait and could not possibly turn and come back for us. Even when the men on board the Kon-Tiki pulled the sail down, the wind pushed the bamboo cabin and drove the balsa raft away to the west as fast as we could follow in the dinghy with its tiny oars. There was only one thought in the head of every man: we must not be separated. Those were bad minutes which we spent on the sea before we reached the raft and crept on board to the others, home again.

From that day it was strictly forbidden to go out in the rubber dinghy without having a rope from the dinghy to the raft, so that the dinghy could be hauled back if necessary. We never went far from the raft, therefore, except when the wind was light and the Pacific calm. Then we could safely row away into the blue space between sea and sky; and when we were far away, a sensation of loneliness sometimes crept over us. We could almost feel that we were hanging in space; all our world was empty and blue. There was no fixed point in it except the sun, which burned our necks, golden and warm. Then the distant sail of the lonely raft drew us back to it; we crept on board and felt that we had come home again to our own world, on board but on firm, safe ground. And inside the cabin we found shade and the scent of bamboos and withered palm leaves.

The cabin was fourteen feet long and eight wide, with a low roof. It gave us a great feeling of safety because in our minds we did not connect a palm-covered bamboo dwelling with sea travel. So the hut made us forget the waves. When we were on board, the bamboo hut and its jungle scent were real, and the sea was like a dream. But it was different in the rubber boat.

Sometimes we sailed out in the rubber boat to look at ourselves by night. The black sea rose on all sides and the stars drew a faint reflection from plankton in the water. We lived, and we felt that intensely. We realized that life had been full for the men of the past also—indeed fuller and richer in many ways than the life of modern man. Before us in the dark the *Kon-Tiki* disappeared completely behind the black masses of water; then she rose again and could be seen clearly against the stars, while water poured from the logs back into the sea.

We could well imagine a large number of such vessels, spread out on the ocean, when the first men crossed the sea. Kon-Tiki and his men had certainly sailed in that way several hundred years before.

When we jumped on board the raft again, we often sat down round the paraffin lamp on the deck and talked of the seafarers from Peru who had had all these same experiences fifteen hundred years before us. The lamp flung enormous shadows of bearded men on the sail, and we remembered the white men with beards who went from Mexico to Central America and into the north-western area of South America as far as Peru. Here the mysterious civilization vanished, and then it reappeared just as suddenly on the lonely islands in the west which we were now approaching. Were those wandering teachers men of an early civilized race from across the Atlantic? Had they come with the ocean current and the trade wind from the Canary Islands to the Gulf of Mexico? That was indeed a much shorter distance than the one we were covering, and we no longer believed that the sea could stop them. Many investigators think that the great Indian civilizations, from the Aztecs in Mexico to the Incas in Peru, were influenced from over the seas in the east, and that the American Indians in general are Asiatic hunting and fishing people, who, in the course of 20,000 years or more, have reached America from Siberia.

And the civilizations have arisen where the current comes in from the Atlantic, in the midst of desert and jungle areas in Central and South America. It is the same in the South Sea islands. It is the island nearest Peru, Easter Island, which has the deepest marks of civilization, although it is dry and barren and is farthest from Asia of all the islands of the Pacific.

When we had completed half our voyage, we had sailed just the distance from Peru to Easter Island. If we had left Peru farther south, we should have got the same wind but a weaker current, both of which would have carried us in the direction of Easter Island.

73

When we passed 110 degrees west, we were within the Polynesian ocean area, because the Polynesian island, Easter Island, was now nearer Peru than we were. We were on a level with the first outpost of the South Sea Islands, the centre of the oldest island civilization. And when, at night, the sun went down and disappeared beyond the sea in the west with its whole spectrum of colours, the gentle trade wind blew life into the strange stories of Easter Island, and the shadows of our bearded heads were again thrown on the sail.

But far away on Easter Island stood larger heads cut in stone with pointed beards and white men's faces. Thus they stood when Europeans first discovered the island in 1722, and thus they stood twenty-two Polynesian generations earlier when the present inhabitants landed there. Since then the enormous stone heads have been among the chief signs of the mysteries of the past. On that treeless island their enormous figures have risen to the sky, beautifully carved in the shape of men, and set up as a single block as high as an ordinary house of three or four floors. How had the men of old time been able to shape, carry and put up such huge stone figures? There is another problem, because they had succeeded in balancing an extra great block of red stone on the top of several of the heads, thirty-six feet above the ground. What did it all mean, and what kind of mechanical knowledge had the vanished builders, who had overcome problems great enough for the best engineers of to-day?

Easter Island is the top of an old volcano, and down inside the opening at the top is the place where those old builders found and cut their stone. It lies there now just as the old artists left it hundreds of years ago, when they escaped in haste to the eastern part of the island. There, according to the story, the newly arrived island people killed every man of them. The old stone axes lie in their working place, and show that the civilized people were as ignorant of iron as Kon-Tiki's men were when they were driven from Peru, leaving stone statues like these behind them in the Andes mountains. In both places the white people with beards cut blocks of stone thirty or forty feet long out of the mountain side with the help of axes of still harder stone. And in both places the stone blocks, weighing many tons, were moved for miles over rough ground before being set up on end as enormous human figures, or raised on top of one another to form mysterious walls.

Many huge unfinished figures still lie where they were begun in their holes on Easter Island, and they show how the work was done in different stages. The largest human figure, which was almost completed when the workers had to run away, was sixty-six feet long; if it had been finished and set up, the head would have been level with the top of an eight-floor building. Every separate figure was hewn out of a single block of stone. The figures on Easter Island were completed in every detail, lying on their backs with their arms bent and their hands placed on their stomachs, before they were removed from the workshop to other parts of the island.

Many of these figures were just dragged down to the bottom of the crater of the volcano, and set up on the slope there. But many were taken farther in some mysterious way. In the Marquesas I heard how the enormous stones were moved.

The work in the pit where the stone was cut took a long time and was done by few men. But large numbers of men were needed to move the stone, although this work was quick. About a thousand men were enough to pull the statues up and over the wall of the crater, and five hundred were enough to drag them farther, across the island. They were dragged with ropes made from plants over logs and stones which had been made slippery.

When a statue reached its proper place, the crowd built an inclined plane, and pulled the figure up the side, legs first. At the top it fell over a sharp edge straight down, so that the feet landed in a ready-made hole. Then they rolled another block of stone up the inclined plane and placed it on top of the head. Inclined planes like this still stand in several places on Easter Island, waiting for the huge figures which have never come.

But why did they make these statues? And why was it necessary to go to another quarry four miles away from the crater workshop to find a special kind of red stone to place on the figure's head? Both in South America and in the Marquesas Islands the whole statue was often of this red stone, and they went great distances to get it. Red head-dresses for people of high rank were important both in Polynesia and Peru.

Let us see whom the statues represented. When the first Europeans visited the island, they saw mysterious white men on shore with long beards. The natives declared that some of their ancestors had been white, and others brown. The brown men had come from other places in Polynesia twenty-two generations before, and the white men had come from the east in large vessels fifty-seven generations

76

before, in about A.D. 400-500. The race which came from the east was given the name "Long-ears" because they lengthened their ears artificially by hanging weights on the bottom parts of them, so that they hung down to their shoulders. These were the mysterious "Long-ears" who were killed when the "Short-ears" came to the island. All the stone figures on Easter Island had large ears hanging down to their shoulders, as their makers had.

The Inca legends in Peru say that the sun-king Kon-Tiki ruled over a white people with beards and big ears, who put up the statues in the Andes mountains before they were killed or driven away.

Thus Kon-Tiki's white "Big-ears" disappeared from Peru to the west and knew how to make enormous statues. And Tiki's white "Long-ears" came to Easter Island from the east and knew exactly the same art.

On all the islands of Polynesia scattered individuals and whole families existed with reddish hair and fair skins, and the islanders said that these were descended from the first white people in the islands. This explains why the statues had red stones on their heads. The stones represented the red hair; the statues were copies of the men who built them.

We used to sit on deck under the starry sky and tell again the strange history of Easter Island, even though our raft was carrying us straight into the heart of Polynesia, so that we should see nothing of that island except its name on the map.

We had no longer the same respect for waves and sea. We knew them and their relationship to us on the raft. Even the shark had become part of the everyday picture.

We did not move away from the side of the raft if a shark came near it. Indeed we were more likely to try to catch hold of it with our hands, and we played games with some of them. We put a bit of fish on the end of a rope in the sea. Just as the shark was going to close its jaws, we pulled the rope away. The shark, with a very foolish expression on its face, swam on and opened its jaws again, but we cheated it once more by pulling the rope away. At last the shark came right up to the logs and jumped up like a dog begging for the food which hung just above its nose.

But our respect for the five or six rows of sharp teeth which lay ready in the shark's enormous jaws never disappeared.

One day Knut had an involuntary swim with a shark. No one was ever allowed to swim away from the raft, but it was unusually calm and Knut plunged in. He was quite a long way off when he came to the surface to return. At that moment we saw, from the top of the mast, a shadow bigger than himself, coming behind him, deeper down. We shouted warnings as softly as we could, and Knut swam hard towards the raft's side. But the shadow belonged to an even better swimmer, which got closer and closer to Knut. They reached the raft at the same time. While Knut climbed on board, a six-foot shark passed gently just under his stomach and stopped beside the raft. We gave it a dolphin's head to thank it for not biting.

Usually it is smell and not sight which attracts sharks. We have sat with our legs in the water to test them, and they have swum towards us and then turned away. But if the water was in the least bloodstained, as it was when we had been cleaning fish, the sharks suddenly collected in large numbers. If we threw out bits of dead shark, they rushed about madly, and if we put a foot into the sea they came straight towards it at a high speed. They even dug their teeth into the wood where the foot had been.

The parrot was quite thrilled when we had a shark on deck. It came out of the cabin and climbed madly up the wall till it found a safe place on the palm-leaf roof. And there it sat, shaking its head with excitement. It was a very good sailor and was always in a good temper. We counted ourselves as seven on board, six of us and the green parrot. We did not count the crab, Johannes, at the stern.

At night the parrot crept into its cage under the roof of the cabin, but in the daytime it marched about the deck or hung on the ropes and did strange exercises. Sometimes when we had all to pull the ropes to tighten them, the parrot called out in its rough voice, "Haul! Haul! ho, ho, ho, ha, ha, ha!" It made us laugh and it laughed itself.

At first the parrot was the enemy of the wireless operators. They might be sitting happily in the wireless corner, wearing earphones, perhaps listening to a wireless amateur in Oklahoma. Then their earphones suddenly became silent and they could not get a sound. The parrot had bitten off the wire of the aerial. This made the wireless operators very angry; but one day the parrot became seriously ill: it had eaten some of the wire. The wireless men were sorry for it then, and became its friends. After that the parrot would sleep nowhere but in the wireless corner.

We enjoyed the parrot's good temper and bright colours for two months, until a big wave came on board. When we discovered that it had taken the parrot into the sea, it was too late. We did not see it, and the *Kon-Tiki* could not be turned or stopped. If anything went overboard from the raft, we had no chance of turning back for it. Numerous experiences had shown that.

The loss of the parrot saddened us the first evening; we knew that exactly the same thing would happen to us if we fell overboard in the night. One careless step, one thoughtless movement, could send us where the green parrot had gone, even in the daylight.

The two wireless operators had had a hard job in their corner since the first day on board. In the Humboldt Current sea water got in, and they had to cover the wireless corner with canvas, to save what could be saved in the high seas. Then they had the problem of fitting a long enough aerial on the little raft. And then they had the trouble with the parrot. In addition to this we were for two weeks in a part of the Humboldt Current where nothing on the wireless could be heard at all because of the effect of the Andes mountains.

But after that Torstein's call sign was heard one night by a wireless amateur in Los Angeles, who was trying to talk to a friend in Sweden. He asked what kind of wireless set we had, and when he got a satisfactory answer, he asked Torstein who he was and where he lived. When he heard that Torstein's dwelling was a bamboo cabin on a raft in the Pacific, there were strange noises until Torstein supplied more details. Then our new friend told us that his name was Hal and his wife's name Anna, and that she was Swedish by birth and would let our families know that we were alive and well.

It was a strange thought for us that evening that a total

stranger called Hal in Los Angeles was the only person in the world except ourselves who knew where we were and that we were well. After that night Hal, whose complete name was Harold Kempel, and his friend Frank Cuevas, took it in turns to sit up every night and listen for signals from the raft. Herman received grateful telegrams from the head of the United States Weather Bureau for his two daily reports from an area for which there were few reports at all. Later Knut and Torstein talked to other radio amateurs almost every night, and these sent on greetings to Norway.

Only for a few days in the middle of the ocean was there too much salt water for the wireless corner, and the station stopped working altogether. The operators toiled day and night with their tools, and all our distant wireless friends thought that the raft's days were ended. But then one night our signal burst out, and several hundred American amateurs replied to the call.

Late one night Knut was working by lamplight in the corner when he suddenly shook me by the leg and said he had been talking to a man who lived just outside Oslo and was called Christian Amundsen. This was a record because the little transmitter did not send out more power than is used by a small electric torch. It was August 2nd, and we had sailed more than 60 degrees round the earth, so that Oslo was at the opposite end of the globe. King Haakon was seventy-five years old the day after, and we sent a message of congratulations direct from the raft. And the day after that we heard Christian again; he sent us a reply from the King, wishing us continued good luck and success on our voyage.

81

We had two cameras on board, and Erik had with him materials for developing photographs on the voyage, so that we could take fresh photographs of things which had not made good pictures. After the whale shark's visit he could not wait any longer, and one evening he developed two films. But the results showed nothing but spots: the film was ruined.

We telegraphed for advice and we were told that our developer was too warm; we must not use a temperature above 60 degrees or the film would be wrinkled.

We sent our thanks and found that the coolest water that we had was in the ocean itself, and that was nearly 80 degrees. Herman was a refrigerating engineer and I told him, as a joke, to get the temperature of the water down to 60 degrees. He did something with a kettle covered with a sleeping bag, and suddenly there was snow on his beard and he showed us a piece of white ice in the kettle.

Erik developed again with splendid results.

After we had entered the area nearer the South Sea islands there was some rain, and the trade wind changed its direction. It had blown steadily and surely from the south-east until we were a good way across; then it moved round more towards due east. We reached our most northerly position on June 10th with latitude 6 degrees, 19 minutes south. We were then so close to the equator that it seemed as if we should sail above even the most northerly islands of the Marquesas group, and disappear completely in the sea without finding land. But then the wind swung round farther, from east to north-east, and drove us down towards the latitude of the world of islands.

If sea and wind were steady, the steering oar was lashed fast, and the *Kon-Tiki*'s sail was filled with wind without any attention. Then the night watch sat in the cabin door and looked at the stars. For if they changed their positions in the sky, it was time for him to go out and see if the steering oar had moved or the wind had turned.

It was easy to steer by the stars. The old Polynesians were great navigators, and steered by the sun in the daytime and the stars at night. Their knowledge of the heavenly bodies was astonishing. They knew that the earth was round, and they had names for the equator and such things. They knew five planets, which they called wandering stars, and they distinguished them from the fixed stars, for which they had nearly two hundred names. A good navigator in old Polynesia knew well in which part of the sky the different stars would rise, and where they would be at different times of the night and on different nights of the year.

Where did the Polynesians obtain their surprising knowledge of the heavens? And where did they obtain their calendar, which was calculated very thoroughly? Certainly not from the Melanesian or Malayan peoples to the west. But the same old vanished civilized race, the "white and bearded men" who had taught Aztecs, Mayas and Incas, had also made a calendar of the same kind, which Europe in those times could not match.

On July 2nd the night watch could no longer sit in peace under the night sky. We had a strong wind and a rough sea, and the raft sailed more quickly than usual. Four men were asleep, Torstein was at the wireless set, and I was steering. Just before midnight I saw some very big breakers behind our stern. They looked like waves which were breaking over a reef, but this was impossible because we had just passed the place. I shouted a warning and turned the raft to take what was coming.

When the first sea reached us, the raft flung her stern up and sideways, and rose over the top of the wave that had just broken. We passed through the boiling foam which poured along both sides of the raft, and the heavy seas rolled by under us. We slid stern first into a broad trough of the waves. Immediately, the next wall of water came and lifted us into the air. The raft was flung sideways to the sea and it was impossible to turn her quickly enough. The next wave began to break into white foam just as it reached us. When it plunged down, the only thing that I could do was to hold tight to the projecting bamboo pole of the cabin roof. There I held my breath as I felt the raft thrown up towards the sky and everything round me carried away in roaring foam. But in a second we and the *Kon-Tiki* were above water again and sliding quietly down the other side of a gentle wave. After that the sea was calm again. The three great waves raced on before us, and behind us lay a line of coconuts in the water.

The last wave had struck the cabin hard, and Torstein was thrown into the wireless corner. The water rushed in and through the wall. On one side of the deck some of the bamboo work was blown open like a crater, and the diving basket was knocked flat. But everything else was as it had been before. We have never been able to explain where the three big waves came from, unless they were due to disturbances on the sea bottom, which are not uncommon in those areas.

Two days later we had our first storm. The wind died away completely, and thick black clouds rolled up from the south. Then there came gusts of wind from the most unexpected directions, so that the steersman was unable to keep control. As quickly as we turned the stern to the new direction of the wind, just as quickly the gusts came at us from another direction and made the sail swing about dangerously. But then the wind started to blow from the direction of the bad weather, and a real storm began.

In an incredibly short time the seas around us were flung up to a height of fifteen feet, and some of the tops of the waves were twenty-five feet above the troughs. When we were in the troughs, the tops were level with our masthead. The wind shook the bamboo wall and whistled through the ropes.

To protect the wireless corner we stretched canvas over the wall of the cabin. Everything loose was firmly lashed, and the sail was taken down. The sea grew dark and unfriendly, and in every direction it was white with breakers. Where the wave-ridges had broken, green patches lay for a long time in the blue-black sea. The wave-tops blew away as they broke, and the drops stood like salt rain over the sea. When the real rain poured over us, the water that ran from our hair and beards tasted salty, while we stumbled about the deck, bending down, naked and frozen, seeing that everything was in order. But the Kon-Tiki took everything that came with ease. The storm became an exciting form of sport, and we all delighted in the fury round us, which the balsa raft overcame so well. She always lay on the wave-tops like a cork, and all the main weight of the water was always a few inches beneath.

Sometimes the waves came so close upon one another that the second reached us while the first was holding the bow up in the air. Then the solid sheets of water thundered in over the steering watch; but the next second the stern went up, and the flood disappeared through the spaces between the logs.

We calculated that in an ordinary calm sea, where there were usually seven seconds between the highest waves, we took in about two hundred tons of water astern in twenty-four hours. We hardly noticed this because it just flowed quietly round the bare legs of the steersman, and just as quietly disappeared again between the logs. But in a heavy storm more than ten thousand tons of water poured on board in twenty-four hours; the helmsman sometimes stood in water up to his waist and felt as if he was forcing his way against the current of a swift river. The raft stood and trembled for a moment, but then the cruel load of water that weighed her down disappeared overboard again.

Herman was out all the time measuring the squalls of gale force. The storm lasted twenty-four hours, and then the wind gradually dropped and we rolled on to the west. To obtain exact measurements Herman had to go up the mast whenever possible, and there he had great difficulty in holding on.

After the storm the fish around us seemed to be infuriated. The water near us was full of sharks, dolphins and other fish. One chased another, and the sea was frequently coloured with thick blood. We decided to catch some of the fish in an attempt to bring order into the chaos around us. Our diary says:

"A six-foot shark was hooked and pulled on board. As soon as the hook was thrown out again, it was swallowed by an eight-foot shark, and we pulled that on board. Then we got a fresh six-foot shark, and we had got it over the edge of the raft when it broke loose and dived. We lost another and then caught one seven feet long. It was now dangerous to stand on the slippery logs fishing, because the three sharks kept throwing up their heads and biting; so we dragged them by the tail into a heap on the foredeck. After that we caught four more sharks."

When we walked about the deck, there were big sharks lying in the way, beating their tails on the deck and trying to bite. We soon had nine lying round us, and we were so tired that we stopped fishing.

Next day there were just as many sharks, and we caught some. But we stopped when we perceived that the sharks' blood which ran off the raft only attracted still more sharks. We threw all the dead bodies overboard and washed the whole deck clean of blood.

When we lay down to sleep on these evenings we thought of greedy sharks' jaws and sharks' blood. I heard one of the men say, for the first time, that it would be pleasant to stretch oneself out comfortably on the green grass on a palm island; he would be glad to see something other than cold fish and rough sea.

The weather had become quite quiet again, but it was never as constant and dependable as before. Gusts of wind brought with them heavy showers of rain, which we were glad to see because a large part of our water supply had begun to go bad. When the rain was pouring down, we collected water from the cabin roof and stood on deck naked and enjoyed the pleasure of having the salt water washed off with fresh water.

On July 21st the wind suddenly died away again. It was hot and still, and we knew from previous experience what this might mean. And we were right. After a few violent gusts from east and west and south, the wind blew from the south, where black clouds had again appeared. Then suddenly Torstein's sleeping bag went overboard. And what happened in the next few seconds took a much shorter time than it takes to tell it.

Herman tried to catch the bag as it went, and fell overboard. I heard a faint cry for help amid the noise of the waves, and saw Herman's head and a waving arm, as well as a vague green object in the water near him. He was struggling to get back to the raft through the high seas. Torstein and I were the first to perceive him, and we felt cold with fear. We cried "Man overboard" as hard as we could. The others had not heard Herman's cry at all because of the noise of the sea, but very soon they were busy on deck. Herman was an excellent swimmer, and although we realized at once that his life was in danger, we hoped that he might be able to reach the edge of the raft before it was too late.

Torstein seized the line which we used for the lifeboat, but this was the only time when it got caught. The whole thing happened in a few seconds. Herman was now level with the stern of the raft, but a few yards away, and his last hope was to reach the end of the steering oar. As he missed the end of the logs he stretched out his arms for the oar, but it slipped away from him. He was now where experience had shown us we could get nothing back.

While Bengt and I put the dinghy into the sea, Knut and Erik threw out the lifebelt on its line. But the wind was so strong that it was just thrown back to the raft. Soon Herman was already far behind the steering oar, swimming as hard as he could to keep up with the raft, while the distance increased with each gust of wind.

Then we suddenly saw Knut plunge into the sea. He had the lifebelt in one hand. He and Herman swam towards each other, and before long both were holding the lifebelt. The dinghy had been pulled back on board; so all four of us took hold of the line to the lifebelt and pulled, with our eyes fixed on the dark object which was just visible behind the two men. This mysterious beast in the water was pushing a big, greenish-black triangle. Only Herman knew that the triangle was a corner of the sleeping bag. But it did not float for very long after we pulled the two men safely on board. Whatever dragged the sleeping bag down into the depths had just missed a better prey.

For a long time afterwards we all felt the coldness of fear. But we were also very thankful that there were still six of us on board. We said a lot of nice things to Knut that day.

There was not much time to think about what had happened. The sky grew black over our heads, the gusts of wind increased in strength, and before night came a new storm was upon us. We made the lifebelt float astern of the raft on a long line, so that we had something behind the steering oar towards which we could swim if we fell overboard.

The storm lasted for five whole days, but after that we saw a glimpse of blue in the sky, and the evil black cloud passed away. The steering oar was smashed and the sail was torn. The centreboards hung loose and banged noisily about, because all the ropes which held them under water were worn through. But we ourselves and our cargo were completely undamaged.

After the two storms the *Kon-Tiki* had become weaker in the joints. The ropes had stretched and had eaten into the balsa wood. We were very glad that we had not used wire ropes, which would have cut the whole raft to pieces in the storms. And if we had used dry balsa wood at the start, the raft would long ago have sunk into the sea under us. It was the sap in the balsa which prevented the sea water from entering all the small holes in the wood.

But now the ropes were so loose that it was dangerous to let one's foot slip down between two logs; for it could be crushed when they came violently together. There came also new and fearful noises from the ropes which held the masts together at the top. We mended the steering oar and the sail. But the centreboards never again became quite what they had been; they did not meet the pressure with their full strength, because they were loose. We could not inspect the ropes underneath because they were covered with seaweed. But, on taking up the whole bamboo deck, we found only three of the main ropes broken. They had been pressed against the cargo, which had worn them away. It was evident that the logs had absorbed a great weight of water, but the cargo was lighter now. Most of our food and water was already used up, and so were the dry batteries for the wireless.

It was clear that we should both float and hold together for the short distance that separated us from the islands ahead. Now another problem appeared: how would the voyage end?

The Kon-Tiki would go on to the westward until she ran her bows into a solid rock or some other fixed object which would stop her. But the voyage would not be ended until all of us were safe on one of the numerous Polynesian islands ahead.

After the last storm it was quite uncertain where the raft would finish her voyage. We were at an equal distance from the Marquesas Islands and the Tuamotu group, and we might easily pass right between these. Each group lay 300 sea miles from us, the Marquesas to the north-west, and the Tuamotu to the south-west. Wind and current were uncertain, but their general direction was due west.

The island which lay nearest to the north-west was Fatuhiva, the little jungle-clad, mountainous island where I had lived in a hut. If the Kon-Tiki landed there, I should meet many acquaintances. But the islands were a long way apart, and we should have to keep our eyes open while we were steering.

But if the raft went towards the Tuamotu group, there the many islands lay close together and covered a wide space of sea. It is a dangerous area, with reefs and palm-covered atolls which rise only six or ten feet above the sea. Reefs surround every atoll, and are a threat to ships.

On July 3rd Nature was able to tell us that there really was land somewhere ahead, although we were still 1,000 sea miles from Polynesia. On and after that day we saw frigate birds (see p. 131); and as they did not come from

America, they must have their homes in another country ahead.

On July 17th we had the first definite visit straight from the islands of Polynesia. Two large boobies (see p. 131) were seen to the west, and soon afterwards they were flying low over our mast. They circled us many times and then settled on the sea beside us. These were the first living messengers that came to welcome us to Polynesia.

For three days and nights we sailed straight towards Fatuhiva, but then a strong north-east wind sent us in the direction of the Tuamotu atolls. We could not longer depend on the ocean currents. One day they were there; another day they were not. Near Polynesia the wind left us to a weak current which alarmed us because its course was in the direction of the Antarctic. But the wind never stopped completely from the beginning of the voyage to the end, and our smallest distance in twenty-four hours was nine sea miles. The average run for the whole voyage was 42½ sea miles in twenty-four hours.

Later the trade wind came back and pushed the raft towards a new and strange part of the world.

One evening large numbers of birds flew away to the west. They were flying home to the nearest island, and we turned the steering oar and set our course in the direction in which they had disappeared.

Next day there were more birds over us, but we did not need to wait for them to show us the way. This time we saw a curious stationary cloud ahead. It rose like a fixed column of smoke, while the other clouds drifted past. The Polynesians, and we also, knew that under such clouds land lay. The sun heats the sand and a stream of warm air rises to the cold air above and makes a cloud.

We steered towards the cloud till it disappeared after sunset. The wind was steady and the *Kon-Tiki* kept on her course easily enough. There was a deafening scream of birds over us all that night, and the moon was nearly full.

Chapter 7

To the south sea islands

ON the night before July 30th there was a new feeling on board the *Kon-Tiki*. Perhaps the cries of the birds reminded us of the earth, after the dead noise of lifeless ropes which was all we had heard above the noise of the sea in the three months behind us. And the moon seemed rounder and larger than ever over the mast. In our fancy it reflected palm-trees and romance; it did not shine with such a yellow light over the cold fishes out in the sea.

At six o'clock Bengt came down from the masthead, woke Herman, and lay down to sleep. Day was beginning when Herman climbed up the mast. Ten minutes later he was down the rope-ladder and was shaking me by the leg.

" Come and look at your island ! "

His face was radiant, and I jumped up, followed by Bengt, who had not quite gone to sleep yet. We climbed up to the place where the masts crossed. There were birds around us, and over to the south-east the red light formed a background for a faint shadow along the edge of the sea.

Land! An island! We stared at it with our eyes and woke the others. They came out sleepily and looked in all directions, as if they thought our bow was just going

94

to run on a beach. And as we watched, the island became clearer.

Our first thought was that it did not lie where it ought to. And it could not have drifted. So the raft must have been caught by a northerly current in the course of the night. We saw from the direction of the waves that we had lost our chance in the darkness. Where we now lay the wind no longer allowed us to press the raft towards the island. There were many different currents in this region and we turned the steering oar; but we knew quite well that it was useless.

At half past six the sun rose out of the sea. The island lay a few sea miles away and seemed to be quite low, with a forest on it. The trees were packed together behind a light-coloured beach, which lay so low that it was frequently hidden by waves. According to Erik's calculations this was Puka-Puka, the first island of the Tuamotu group.

We were silent after the oar was turned. At last we had proof that we had really been moving all these months; we had not been just lying about in the middle of the same endless, circular sea. We were all filled with warm satisfaction because we had really reached Polynesia; but we were faintly disappointed when we saw the island lie there like a mirage while we continued our endless drift to the west.

Just after sunrise a thick black column of smoke rose above the tree-tops to the left of the middle of the island. We had no idea then that the natives had seen us and were sending up smoke signals to invite us to land. About seven o'clock we smelt the faint scent of burnt wood, which awoke in me slumbering memories of the fire on the beach on Fatuhiva. Half an hour later we caught the smell of newly cut wood and of forest. The island was now getting smaller behind us, so that we received little breezes from it. This was Polynesia—a beautiful rich smell of dry land after ninety-three salty days among the waves. Bengt was already asleep again. Erik and Torstein lay in the cabin thinking, and Knut ran in and out, smelling the leaves and writing in his diary.

At half past eight Puka-Puka sank into the sea astern of us, but till eleven o'clock there was a faint blue streak in the east. Then that too was gone, and a high cloud was all that showed where Puka-Puka lay. The birds disappeared, the dolphins were scarcer, and there were only a few pilot fish under the raft.

That night Bengt said that he longed for a table and chair, for it was tiring to lie and turn from back to stomach when reading. But he was glad that we had missed the island, because he had still three books to read.

The next morning we saw more clouds. The map told us that the names of the coral islands they came from were Fangahina and Angatau. The cloud over Angatau was the more favourable for us, so we set our course for that, and enjoyed the wonderful peace and freedom of the Pacific. We drank in all the impressions, feeling certain that the journey would soon be over now.

For three days and nights we steered towards Ångatau. On the fourth morning Herman said that he thought he had seen the outlines of a low island in the moonlight. Torstein took his place, and when the sun rose just afterwards, he shouted "Land ahead!"

We all ran out on deck and what we saw made us put up all our flags. The island was right in our course, and as the sun rose we could see a green reflection high up over the island. It was the reflection of the green lagoon on the inside of the surrounding reef.

About ten o'clock we could distinguish individual tree-tops and rows of tree-trunks.

We knew that between us and the island was a danger-ous submerged reef. The waves broke over it in thunder and foam. Many vessels have been caught in these waves and broken to pieces against the coral.

From the sea we could see nothing of this dangerous trap. We sailed in, following the waves. The reef was hidden behind them, but along both ends of the island a few hundred yards from land we saw that the sea was one white boiling mass, flinging itself high into the air.

At noon we could see that on the shore grew young green coconut palms, and on the beach in front of them a number of large coral blocks lay about on the bright sand.

We had come so close at two o'clock that we began to sail along the island, just outside the reef. As we gradu-ally approached, we heard the roar of the breakers and soon they sounded like an express train running parallel with us a few hundred yards away.

Two men steered together; they were behind the bam-boo cabin and so had no view ahead whatever. Erik gave directions from the top of the box. Our plan was to keep as close to the dangerous reef as was safe, and we watched for an opening where we could try to slip the raft through.

The current was driving us along the reef and it played no tricks upon us. Erik directed the raft sometimes towards the reef and then away from it.

Herman and I went out in the rubber dinghy at the end of the rope. When the raft was sailing towards the reef, we swung after her on the rope and came so close to the thundering waves that we saw the naked reef itself when the water rolled away from it. We could see no gap or opening, so Erik turned the raft away from the danger till her next drive inwards.

Each time the *Kon-Tiki* was near the reef, we two in the dinghy were filled with keen anxiety. But each time Erik turned the raft away with great skill, and the *Kon-Tiki* ran out to the open sea again. And all the time we were passing the island, so close that we saw every detail on the shore. Yet we could not reach the heavenly beauty because of the foaming reef which lay between.

About three o'clock we looked right into a blue glassy lagoon. But the surrounding reef was as compact as ever. There was no passage.

All day we turned to and fro along Angatau, and had its beauty just outside the cabin door. The sun beat down on the palms, and all was joy on the island. Erik got out his guitar and stood on deck in a huge Peruvian sun-hat playing and singing love songs of the South Seas, while Bengt served an excellent dinner on the edge of the raft. The peace over the bright green forest of palms, the peace over the white birds that flew around the palm-tops, the peace over the soft sand beach, and the fierceness of the red reef, the thunder and the sound of drums in the air, made an enormous impression on the six of us who had come in from the sea. We shall never forget it. There was no doubt now that we had reached the other side; we should never see a more genuine South Sea island. Whether we landed or not, we had reached Polynesia; the stretch of open sea lay behind us for ever.

This was the ninety-seventh day on board. In New York we had calculated that ninety-seven days were the minimum time in which we could reach the islands of Polynesia.

About five o'clock we passed two huts with palm roofs which lay among the trees on shore. But there was no smoke and no sign of life.

At half past five we approached the reef again; we were getting near the west end of the island now, and we must have a last look in the hope of finding a passage. On the beach inside we detected a number of black spots. Suddenly one of them moved slowly down towards the water, and several others ran away at full speed to the edge of the woods. They were people! We steered along the reef as close as we dared, and then we saw some men putting a canoe into the sea. Two of them jumped in and rowed away on the other side of the reef. Farther down they turned the boat's head out and we saw the canoe lifted high in the air as it shot through a passage in the reef and came straight towards us.

The two men in the canoe waved. We waved back eagerly and they increased their speed. It was a Polynesian outrigger canoe.

Now there would be fresh language difficulties. I alone of those on board remembered a few words of Marquesan from my stay on Fatuhiva, but Polynesian is a difficult language to remember because one hardly ever gets any practice in our northern countries.

We felt some relief, therefore, when the canoe touched the raft's side and the two men jumped on board; for one of them laughed, held out a brown hand, and exclaimed in English:

" Good night! "

" Good night! " I replied with astonishment. " Do you speak English? "

The man laughed again and nodded.

" Good night," he said. " Good night."

This was his entire vocabulary in foreign languages!

" Angatau? " I asked, pointing towards the island.

" H'angatau," the man nodded.

Erik nodded proudly. He had been right. We were where the sun had told him we were.

" *Maimai hee iuta,*" I tried. According to my knowledge obtained on Fatuhiva, this should mean " want to go to land ".

Both men pointed towards the invisible passage in the reef. We turned the oar to take our chance.

At that moment gusts of wind came from the island, and threatened to force us away from the reef. We saw that the *Kon-Tiki* was not answering the steering oar at a wide enough angle to be able to reach the mouth of the opening through the reef. We tried to drop an anchor, but we could not find bottom. The anchor rope was not long enough. We pulled down the sail as fast as we could and each of us got out his big paddle. I wanted to give an extra paddle to each of the two natives, who stood enjoying the cigarettes we had given them.

The natives only shook their heads, pointed the way, and looked puzzled. I made signs that we must all paddle, and repeated the words "want to go to land!" Then one of the two bent down, made a turning motion with his right hand, and said:

"Brrrrrrrr——"

There was no doubt whatever that he wanted us to start the engine. They thought we had an engine, so we took them to the stern and showed them that we had not. They were absolutely astonished, and flung themselves down on the side of the raft; there we sat, four men on each side, digging our paddles into the water. At the same time the sun set and the gusts of wind freshened. We did not seem to be moving an inch. The natives looked frightened, jumped back into the canoe, and disappeared. It grew dark and we were alone once more.

As darkness fell over the island, four canoes came out from behind the reef, and soon there was a crowd of Polynesians on board, all wanting to shake hands and get cigarettes. They had local knowledge and we thought there was no danger. They would not let us go out to sea again; we should be on shore that evening!

We quickly fixed ropes from the sterns of all the canoes to the bow of the *Kon-Tiki*. They rowed and pulled, and we others paddled on the raft. Knut jumped into the dinghy and went among the canoes. And so began for the first time a struggle against the east wind.

On land the inhabitants had lighted a fire to show us the way through the reef. We could not see the men in the canoes ahead, but we heard them singing. We could hear that Knut was with them, for whenever the Polynesian music died away we heard Knut's solitary voice singing Norwegian songs. We on the raft also sang, and both brown and white men heaved at their paddles with laughter and song.

Ninety-seven days! We had arrived in Polynesia. The natives cheered and shouted. There was a landing on Angatau only once a year, when a ship came from Tahiti for copra. So there would indeed be a feast round the fire on land that evening.

But the angry wind blew stubbornly. We worked till every limb ached. We did not move backwards, but the fire did not come any nearer, and the thunder from the reef was just the same as before. Gradually the singing stopped. All grew still. Three hours passed and it was now nine o'clock. Gradually we began to go backwards. We were tired.

We made the natives understand that we needed more help from the land, but they explained that they had only these four sea-going canoes.

Then Knut appeared out of the darkness with the dinghy. He had an idea: he could row in the dinghy and fetch more natives. He could bring five or six men crowded together in the dinghy.

But I thought this was too risky. Knut had no local knowledge; he would never be able to get through the passage in the reef. He then proposed to take with him the leader of the natives, who could show him the way. I did not think this plan safe either, for the native had no experience in taking a clumsy rubber dinghy through the narrow and dangerous passage. But I asked Knut to fetch the leader, who was paddling in the darkness ahead of us, so that we might hear what he thought. It was clear that we were no longer able to prevent ourselves from drifting astern.

Knut went to find the leader. Some time passed and he did not return, so we shouted for them but received no answer except a chorus in Polynesian ahead. At that moment we understood what had happened. Knut had misunderstood his instructions and had rowed towards the shore with the leader. All our shouts were useless, for all other sounds were drowned by the thunder of the reef.

We got a lamp and signalled, "Come back! Come back!"

But no one came back.

Our drift backwards increased; we were all really tired. The fire grew smaller, the noise from the breakers less. And as we slowly left the shelter of the palm forest, the wind took a firmer hold of us. We gradually realized that all hope had gone: we were drifting out to sea. But we must paddle hard to make the drift as slow as possible, till Knut was safe on board again.

The breakers became a distant murmur, and the fire sometimes disappeared behind the waves. We heard the natives beginning to complain, and suddenly we noticed that one of the canoes had disappeared. The men in the other three were tired and frightened, and were no longer pulling well.

Soon the three canoes came back to the raft. One of the natives came on board and said:

"*Iuta.*" (To land.)

We gave them cigarettes, and I hastily scrawled a note

for them to take with them to Knut if they found him.
It said:

"Take two natives with you in a canoe pulling the
dinghy. Do *not* come back in the dinghy alone."

It would be madness for Knut to go out on the ocean in
the dinghy alone, in the hope of reaching the raft.

The natives took the scrap of paper, jumped into the
canoes, and disappeared into the night. The last we heard
was the voice of our friend in the darkness, calling politely:

"Good night!"

Then all was silent.

We on the raft sent regular flashes with our signal lamp,
but at ten o'clock we lost the last faint hope of seeing
Knut again. We decided to signal with the lamp all night,
so long as we did not know where Knut was. We refused
to believe that he had been caught by the breakers. Knut
always took care of himself; he was alive. But it was very
annoying that he was stuck on a small island alone with
Polynesians. After all that long voyage, all we could do
was to land a man on an island and then sail away again.

At half past ten we all started: we heard the voices of
Polynesians on the sea. We shouted back into the night
with all the strength of our lungs, and then we heard
Knut's voice among the rest! We were mad with excitement, and our tiredness disappeared. What did it matter
if we drifted away from Angatau? There were other
islands in the sea. It did not matter so long as all six of
us were together on board again.

Three outrigger canoes arrived, and Knut was the first
to jump on board. Six natives followed. There was little
time for explanations, for they had to go back on their

dangerous journey to the island. But they were obviously anxious about us. They pointed to the west and explained that we were heading towards dangerous reefs. The leader had tears in his eyes and kissed me, which made me thankful for my beard. Then they left in their canoes.

Knut told us his story. He had misunderstood me and set out for the land with the leader of the natives. Then Knut was surprised to see the signals from the raft telling him to come back. He told the native to turn, but the man refused. They started to struggle, but with the reef so near it was foolish to fight. They passed through the opening and reached the island. A crowd of natives dragged the dinghy ashore. Brown, bare-legged men, women and children flocked round Knut, and he made signs to some of them that they should go out in the dinghy with him.

Then a fat man came. Knut supposed him to be the chief, for he wore a cap on his head and spoke importantly. Knut explained both in Norwegian and in English that he needed men and must go back to the raft before it drifted away. But the chief smiled and understood nothing, and Knut was taken to the village by the crowd. There he was received by dogs and pretty South Sea girls, who brought fresh fruit. But Knut was not ready to be enticed. He thought sadly of the raft, which was disappearing in the west.

The natives' intention was obvious. They knew that there were many good things on board white men's ships and they wanted us to come ashore. If they could keep Knut there, the rest of us would surely come. No vessel would leave a white man on Angatau.

After some curious experiences, Knut got away and hurried to the dinghy, surrounded by admirers of both sexes. They understood him now. They realized that he must go. Then the three canoes came back and brought Knut my note, and he did not know what to do; for he was told not to row out on the sea alone, and the natives absolutely refused to go with him.

After a violent argument among the natives, the crews of three canoes agreed to go with him out to sea. They set out with the dinghy behind, while the other natives stood by the dying fire and watched their new friend disappear into the night. And so Knut came back.

"Did you have a good time ashore?" Torstein asked enviously.

"Oh, you should have seen the girls!" said Knut.

For three days we drifted across the sea, without sight of land, towards the dangerous Takume and Raroia reefs, which together blocked up forty to fifty miles of the sea ahead of us. We tried hard to steer away to the north of these reefs; but one night the wind changed and drove us straight towards the Takume reef. It had begun to rain and we could not see well, but the reef could not be far off.

In the middle of the night we held a conference. It was a question of saving our lives now. We could not get past the north side; we must try the south instead. We began a dangerous piece of sailing with the north wind behind us. If the east wind came back before we had passed the whole of the reef, we should be thrown in among the breakers.

We agreed about all that must be done if shipwreck was coming. We would stay on board whatever happened.

We would not climb up the mast, but hold to the ropes when the sea poured over us. We laid the rubber raft loose on deck, and fastened on it a small wireless set, and some provisions and water. This would be washed ashore independently. In the stern of the *Kon-Tiki* we fixed a long rope with a float. This would also be washed ashore, so that we could try to pull the raft in if she were lost on the reef. And so we crept into bed.

One afternoon the wind fell, and when it came back it had gone round into the east. We were already so far down now that we had some hope of passing the southern-most point of the Raroia reef. When night came we had been a hundred days at sea.

At dawn, just before six o'clock, Torstein said he could see a whole line of palm-clad islands ahead. We laid the oar over to the south as far as we could.

The most southerly island lay roughly ahead of our bows, and the rest disappeared as dots away to the north. The nearest were four or five sea miles away, and we were drifting right towards the reef. With fixed centreboards we should have had some hope of steering clear. But they were loose and we could not dive under the raft and fix them with new ropes, because of sharks.

We saw that we had now only a few more hours on board the *Kon-Tiki*, and we must use them to prepare for our inevitable shipwreck. Each of us learnt his own duty as the wind forced us in. We saw from the mast how all the islands were connected with a coral reef, part above and part under the water. The whole of the longer side of Raroia faces the sea to the east, where we were coming in. The reef itself, which runs in one line from horizon to horizon, is only a few hundred yards from the small islands behind.

Everything of value was carried into the cabin and lashed fast. Papers were packed into bags, and the whole bamboo cabin was covered with canvas. We pulled up the centreboards so that we might be more easily washed over the reef. But without them the raft was entirely at the mercy of wind and sea.

The main order was: Hold on to the raft. We must not jump overboard when we struck the reef, and we could not use the rubber raft because it would be torn to pieces on the coral. But the wooden logs of the *Kon-Tiki* would reach the shore sooner or later, and we with them.

We put on our shoes for the first time in a hundred days and got our lifebelts ready. These were anxious hours as we drifted helplessly towards the reef, but we had confidence in our raft.

Entries in the log-book were:

8.15. We are slowly approaching land. We can now see separate palm trees.

8.45. The wind is even more unfavourable than before, so we have no hope of getting clear. We think we can see the wreck of a sailing vessel on the reef.

9.45. The wind is taking us straight towards an island behind the reef. All along the reef foaming surf is flung up towards the sky. Bengt is serving a good hot meal, the last before the great action! It *is* a wreck on the reef.

9.50. Very close now. Only a hundred yards away. It looks bad, but we shall succeed.

A few minutes later the anchor rushed overboard, so that the *Kon-Tiki* swung round and turned her stern towards the reef where the breakers thundered. Torstein got a message through to Rarotonga by wireless and said we were drifting towards the Raroia reef. He asked them to listen every hour and said that, if we were silent for more than thirty-six hours, they must tell the Norwegian Embassy in Washington.

We were ready, and each of us held fast to the rope which he thought best. When we realized that the seas had got hold of us, we cut the anchor rope and we were off! We felt the *Kon-Tiki* lifted up into the air. The great moment had come. The excitement made one's blood boil.

A new sea rose behind us like a green glass wall; as we sank down it came rolling after us. I felt a violent blow and was submerged under floods of water. I had to use every muscle in my body to hold on. Then I felt the mountain of water passing on and relaxing its hold. I looked round and saw that the others were safe.

We were still floating!

Another green wall of water came towards us and in an instant the *Kon-Tiki* disappeared under it. The sea pulled with all its force on our little human bodies. The second sea rushed over us, and a third like it.

Knut gave a triumphant shout: "Look at the raft! She's holding!"

The mast and the cabin had been knocked a bit crooked, but the raft was winning the battle.

In the next wave I myself disappeared sideways; the others estimated the height of the wave as twenty-five feet. We must have hit the reef that time. I was under water only a few seconds, but it needed more strength than we usually have in our bodies to hold on. The sea thundered past, and after it was gone I saw a terrible sight. The *Kon-Tiki* was wholly changed; in a few seconds she had become a shattered wreck.

I saw only one man on board besides myself. This was Herman, pressed flat on the cabin roof, while the cabin itself was crushed together towards the stern. There the steering block was twisted round and partly broken and the oar was smashed to bits. The whole bamboo deck was torn up and pressed against the front wall of the cabin.

I was afraid. What was the use of holding on? But then Torstein's figure appeared, hanging like a monkey on a rope. Then I heard Bengt's calm voice calling that everyone was on board. They were all behind the remains of the bamboo deck.

I saw the ends of the logs knocking against a sharp step on the reef without going over it. We were all very discouraged. When the next sea had passed I was dead tired. I saw for the first time the rough red reef beneath us. Torstein was on the coral, holding a bunch of ropes from the mast, and Knut was about to jump off. I shouted that we must all stay on the logs, and Torstein jumped on board again.

I do not remember what happened then, except that I myself sank lower and lower towards the red reef over which we were being lifted. But soon we were all able to reach the stern of the raft, which was highest up on the reef.

Knut sprang on the reef with the rope from the stern,

went thirty yards in, and stood safely at the end of the rope. Then Erik came out of the cabin. He had been lucky there, pressed down flat under the canvas. Bengt had slight concussion, but he had managed to creep into the cabin with Erik.

Erik, Herman and Bengt jumped on the reef. When Torstein's turn and my own came, the raft lay far in on the reef, and we began to save what we could.

We were now twenty yards away from that devilish step up on the reef. The atoll was so high that only the tops of the breakers were able to drive water past us into the lagoon behind.

The others found the rubber raft full of water. After emptying it they took it back to the raft and loaded it with the radio set, provisions and water. We dragged all this to a huge block of coral inside the reef, and went back for fresh loads.

Where we had stranded, we had only pools of water and wet coral about us, and the calm lagoon lay farther in. The tide was going out. What would happen on the narrow reef when it came in again was uncertain. We must get away.

At the south end of the reef was a long island thickly covered with palm forest; but to the north lay a smaller island with palms and sandy beaches, and this was the island which we chose.

I took a last look at the wreck and began to wade towards the island. I saw Knut happily on the way, and Bengt pushing a box in which were the Primus stove and the cooking utensils.

When I reached the sunny beach, I slipped off my shoes

and thrust my toes into the warm dry sand. I enjoyed the sight of every footprint. Soon the palm tops closed over my head as I went on, right towards the centre of the small island. Green coconuts hung in the trees, and some of the flowers on the bushes smelt so sweet that I felt quite faint. I was overwhelmed. I sank down on my knees and thrust my fingers down into the sand.

The voyage was over. We were all alive. We had run on an uninhabited South Sea island. And what an island!

Soon we were all six lying on our backs and looking up at the palms and the birds. Herman climbed a tree and brought down some green coconuts. We cut off their soft tops and poured down our throats the most refreshing drink in the world: sweet cold milk from young palm fruit.

And as we lay and stretched ourselves, the breakers outside thundered like a train, to and fro, to and fro, all along the horizon.

This was heaven.

Chapter 8

Among Polynesians

WE soon learnt to know every detail of our uninhabited island. It was hardly two hundred yards across and the highest point was only six feet above the lagoon.

To the north we could see another small island far away, but the island to the south was much closer. We saw no sign of life on either.

After a meal we put together the wireless apparatus. We had to be quick, so that Torstein and Knut might tell the man at Rarotonga of our safety before he sent out a report of our sad end.

While the operators were busy at the wireless set, we others made a tent with the sail from the wreck. Then over our heads we saw the big bearded face of good old Kon-Tiki. We put out many things to dry in the sun, and the wireless operators too had to wait until the sun had dried the inside of their apparatus.

When we awoke the next morning the sail was full of clear rain-water, and fish provided food for breakfast. That night Herman had pains in the neck where he had damaged himself before the start from Lima, and Bengt still had slight concussion. Otherwise none of us had suffered much in the shipwreck.

The sea was a marvellous world in which we could swim and enjoy ourselves. But we could not stay long in it; we must make the wireless work in time to stop news of our death from reaching the world.

Wireless parts lay drying in the tropical sun. The whole day passed and we all left our other jobs and crowded round the wireless men in the hope of being able to help. We must send a message before 10 p.m. If we did not, our wireless friend on Rarotonga would send out appeals for aeroplanes and relief expeditions.

Noon came, afternoon came, and the sun set. Nine o'clock! Not a sign of life in the transmitter, but the receiver gave us a little faint music.

We tried another little transmitter which we had. Seven minutes more! Five minutes more! The transmitter was as dead as ever. But the receiver was working now, and we heard a bit of our friend's message:

". . . no aeroplane this side of Samoa. I am quite sure. . . ."

What were they doing there? Had they already sent out an aeroplane to rescue us? Our two operators worked feverishly. Sweat fell from their faces. Slowly power came into the transmitter. It was beginning to work!

Torstein called Rarotonga, but no one heard us. Once more. No one heard us!

Then Torstein sent out a message to all stations in the world and we heard a reply in a faint voice:

"My name is Paul and I live in Colorado. Who are you and where do you live?"

Torstein answered: "This is the *Kon-Tiki*; we are on a desert island in the Pacific."

Paul did not believe this information at all. He thought that someone was playing a joke and he did not answer. We were in despair.

Torstein sent out, "All well, all well, all well," continuously. We must try to stop the rescue which was being started.

Then we heard faintly in the receiver, "If all's well, why worry?" Then the voice stopped. That was all.

But suddenly good old Hal heard us. He was delighted to know we were safe. All the noise stopped immediately and we went to bed.

On the next day we planted a coconut from Peru opposite the place where the *Kon-Tiki* had run ashore. Erik and Herman were anxious to go to the south along the reef towards the large island that lay there. I warned them against eels and they took knives with them. These eels have long poisonous teeth which can tear off a man's leg, and they are feared by the natives, who are not afraid of sharks.

The two men waded over long stretches of reef southward, but sometimes they had to swim. They reached the big island safely and went to its southern point, from where the reef stretched to other islands. They found the wreck of a big ship there, an old Spanish sailing vessel. But they found no tracks in the sand.

On the way back they were attacked by eight large eels, and they jumped on a block of coral. The eels were as thick as a man's leg, and were spotted green and white like poisonous snakes. The men cut off the head of one and injured another. The blood in the sea attracted sharks, which attacked the dead and injured eels, while Erik and

Herman jumped to another block of coral and escaped. On the same day I myself was attacked by a cuttle-fish in the water, and only when I reached the edge of the dry sand did it let go.

We enjoyed life on the island, but we had to think of how we should reach the outer world again. After a week the *Kon-Tiki* had bumped her way to the middle of the reef, where she lay on dry land; but all our pulling and pushing could not move her farther. We wanted to sail in her to one of the other islands; and if any of them were inhabited, it must be that which lay to the west, where the atoll turned its face towards the sheltered side.

The days passed, and then some of the men saw two white sails in the lagoon. They grew in size as the morning went on, and they came straight towards us. We put up our flags.

One of the sails was now so near that we could see that it belonged to a Polynesian outrigger canoe. Two brown figures stood on board gazing at us. We waved and they waved back.

We greeted them in Polynesian and were answered by shouts. One man jumped out and dragged his canoe after him as he waded over the sandy shallows towards us.

The two men had white men's clothes but brown men's bodies, and they wore hats to protect them from the sun. They approached us uncertainly, but when we smiled they smiled back.

They thought that we understood a lot of Polynesian and spoke quickly for a long time before they saw that we did not. Then they could do nothing but laugh and point to the other canoe which was approaching.

There were three men in this, and one of them could speak a little French. We learnt that there was a native village on one of the islands across the lagoon, and from it the Polynesians had seen our fire several nights earlier. There was only one passage through the reef to the circle of islands round the lagoon, and this passage ran right past the village. So no vessel could approach these islands inside the reef without being seen by the inhabitants. The old people in the village, therefore, had decided that the light they saw to the east could not be the work of man, but must be supernatural. This had quenched all desire to go and look at it.

But then part of a box had drifted across the lagoon. Two of the natives were able to read TIKI in big black letters on the wood. Then there was no longer any doubt that there were spirits on the reef, for Tiki was the long-dead founder of their race. They all knew that. But after that bread, cigarettes and cocoa in tins had drifted across the lagoon, and they realized that there had been a shipwreck. So the chief sent two canoes to look for survivors.

We explained to them that "Kon-Tiki" was on all our equipment, and that it was the name of our vessel. Our new friends were astonished when they heard that everyone on board had been saved, and that the flat wreck on the reef was our vessel. They wanted to take us at once to their village in their canoes. We thanked them and refused, as we wanted to stay until we got the Kon-Tiki off the reef. They did not believe that we could do that, and finally the spokesman said that we must go with them. The chief had ordered them not to return without us.

After some discussion Bengt went with them, and was told to come back and report to us about conditions on the island.

Next day the horizon was crowded with white sails, and when the canoes were nearer we saw Bengt waving his hat in the first. He shouted to us that the chief was with him, and we waited respectfully on the beach.

Bengt presented us to the chief with great ceremony. His name was Tepiuraiarii Teriifaatau, but he would understand whom we meant if we called him Teka. We did call him Teka.

Teka was a tall, thin Polynesian with intelligent eyes, and was chief of both the Raroia and the Takume islands. He had been to school in Tahiti, so that he spoke French and could both read and write. He told us that only three foreign vessels had called at Raroia in the last ten years, but that the village was visited several times a year by a schooner from Tahiti. They had been expecting her for several weeks now, and so she might come at any time.

Bengt said that there was no school, wireless or white man on Raroia, but that the 120 Polynesians were preparing to welcome us. The chief wanted to look at the *Kon-Tiki* and so we waded out to her with a crowd of natives.

"That's not a boat; it's a *pae-pae*!" cried one of them. "*Pae-pae!*" they all repeated together.

They clambered on board the raft like excited children and felt the logs, the bamboos and the ropes. The chief was in high spirits like the others. He came back and repeated, "The *Tiki* isn't a boat; she's a *pae-pae*."

Pae-pae is the Polynesian word for raft. The chief told us that *pae-paes* no longer existed. All the men admired

119

the logs, but not the ropes. Ropes like those did not last many months, in salt water and sun. They proudly showed us their own lashings, made from coconut hemp, and told us that they remained good for five years at sea.

When we waded back, our little island was named Kon-Tiki Island. This was a name we could all pronounce, but our brown friends found our northern names hard to pronounce. They were delighted when I said they could call me Terai Mateata, a name given to me by the great chief in Tahiti.

We had to tell all our experiences with the raft at sea, and they wanted to hear about the whale shark again and again. They recognized at once all the fish when we showed them drawings of them, and gave us their names in Polynesian. But they had never seen or heard of the whale shark.

When the evening came we delighted them all by turning on the wireless. They liked the music best, and some of them began to dance to hula-hula music from America. After that we all slept round the fire.

The next morning there was more thunder than usual on the reef.

"The *Tiki*'ll come in to-day," said the chief, pointing to the wreck. "There'll be high tide."

About eleven o'clock the sea rose all round the island. The masses of water tore away huge coral blocks. Loose bamboos from the wreck sailed past us, and the *Kon-Tiki* began to move. Everything that was lying on the beach had to be carried away, so that it might not be caught by the rising tide. The sea rose and rose, and we began to feel anxious. It looked as if the whole ocean were invading us. The *Kon-Tiki* swung right round and drifted until she was caught by some coral blocks.

The natives swam to the raft, and Knut and Erik followed. Ropes lay ready on board, and when she broke loose from the reef, the natives tried to hold her. They did not know the *Kon-Tiki* and her ungovernable urge to move westward. So they were towed with her helplessly, and she was soon moving at a good speed right across the reef and into the lagoon. The natives succeeded in tying the end of the rope round a palm on land, and there the *Kon-Tiki* hung, tied up fast in the lagoon. The craft that went over land and water had crossed the reef into the lagoon.

We pulled her to the shore of the island of her own name.

The waves were breaking all over the lagoon, and we could not get much equipment into the narrow canoes. The natives had to go back to the village in a hurry, and Bengt and Herman went with them to see a small boy who lay dying in a hut. The boy had an abscess on his head and we had penicillin.

Next day we four were alone on Kon-Tiki Island. The east wind was now so strong that the natives could not cross the lagoon. But on the following day it was quieter again. We were able to dive under the *Kon-Tiki* and see that the nine logs were intact, though the reef had taken an inch or two off the bottom. The ropes were so deep in the grooves that only four had been cut by the corals. We began to clear up the deck, pulled the cabin out again, and mended the mast.

Sails appeared on the horizon during the day; the

natives were coming to fetch us and the rest of the cargo. Herman and Bengt were with them and told us that the natives had prepared a great feast in the village.

We sailed across the lagoon, which was here seven miles wide. We said good-bye to Kon-Tiki Island with real sorrow. But ahead of us larger islands were appearing, and on one of them we saw a jetty and smoke rising from huts among the palms.

The village looked quite dead; not one person could be seen. What was going to happen now? On the beach, behind a jetty of coral blocks, stood two lonely figures, one tall and thin and one big and fat. As we came in, we saluted them both. They were the chief, Teka, and the vice-chief, Tupuhoe. We all liked Tupuhoe's broad smile. Teka was intelligent, but Tupuhoe was a child of nature. With his powerful body and kingly face, he was exactly like our ideas of a Polynesian chief. He was indeed the real chief on the island, but Teka had gradually reached the most important position because he could speak French and count and write, and this was useful when the schooner came from Tahiti to fetch copra.

Teka explained that we must march together to the meeting-house in the village, and so we set out, Herman first with the flag, and then I myself between the two chiefs.

Some of the huts of the village were of the old kind, but others were fastened together with nails, brought by the schooner. A large house, standing alone among the palms, was the new meeting-house; there we six white men were to stay. We marched in with the flag through a small back door, and out to some steps. Before us stood everyone in the village who could walk or crawl, women and children, old and young, and all were very serious.

When we had come out on the steps, the whole crowd began to sing the Marseillaise. Teka, who knew the words, led the singing, and the others followed fairly well. The flags were hoisted in front of the steps, and then Teka went quietly away. Now the fat Tupuhoe sprang forward and gave a quick sign, after which another song began. This was in their own language and was sung better. The music was so attractive and simple that we had a strange feeling down our backs as the South Sea roared towards us. The music of the song changed a little, but the words were always the same:

"Good day, Terai Mateata and your men, who have come across the sea on a *pae-pae* to us on Raroia. Yes, good day. May you remain long among us and share memories with us so that we can always be together, even when you go away to a far land. Good day."

We asked them to sing the song again, and more life came into them as they grew more accustomed to us. Then Tupuhoe asked me to speak to the crowd. I must speak in French and Teka would translate.

So I told them that I had been in the South Sea islands before, and that I had heard of their first chief, Tiki, who had brought their ancestors from a mysterious country. I said that no one knew which country. But in a distant land called Peru a great chief ruled whose name was Tiki, and he had at last disappeared with his men on big *pae-paes*. Therefore we thought that he was the same Tiki who came to the islands, and as nobody would believe that a *pae-pae* could cross the sea, we ourselves had set out from Peru on a *pae-pae,* and here we were. So it could be done.

After the speech Tupuhoe sprang forward in front of the assembly and talked so fast that we could not understand what he said. But the crowd was visibly excited. Teka had to translate for us.

Tupuhoe had said that his ancestors had spoken of Tiki, but then white men came and said that these traditions were all lies. But now we six agreed that their ancestors had spoken the truth. Tiki had been real, but now he was dead and in heaven.

I did not want them to think that Tiki was a god, and so I said that he was certainly dead; but whether he was in heaven or not, we did not know.

While the old men wanted to discuss Tiki, the young ones wanted to hear about the whale shark. But the food was waiting and Teka was tired of translating.

Now the whole village shook hands with us. Everyone was friendly. A long table was laid for the two chiefs and us six, and the village girls brought delicious food. While some arranged the table, others hung flowers round our necks. And so a feast of welcome began which did not end till we left the island weeks afterwards. While we ate the many kinds of food, the crowd sang hula-hula songs, and young girls danced round the table.

After the meal there was hula dancing on a grand scale. There were two rows of dancing men and women, and a singer whose arm had been bitten off by a shark. Later some of the older people joined in the dance, and as the sun set over the Pacific it became more and more lively. They had forgotten that we who sat among them were six strangers; we were now six of their own people, enjoying ourselves with them.

This was the South Sea life as the old days had known it. The stars twinkled and the palms waved. The night was mild and long and full of the scent of flowers. Even Teka thought that it was a very good feast. It was the first time white men had been present on Raroia, he said. Faster and faster went the drums, the singing and the dancing.

Now one of the girls stretched out her arms to Herman. "Go on," I whispered. "You're a good dancer."

The crowd was delighted when Herman sprang forward and began to dance. Soon Bengt and Torstein joined in. Now the evening was ours; there was no end to the enthusiasm. When I myself started, I saw old Tupuhoe laughing so much that he nearly fell down on the ground.

The feast continued till daylight. Then six beds were placed together along the wall in the meeting-house, and in them we slept, with sweet-smelling flowers hanging above our heads.

Next day the boy of six who had an abscess on his head seemed worse. His temperature was nearly 106 degrees, and the abscess was as large as a man's fist. We did not know how much penicillin we ought to give him.

Knut and Torstein talked by wireless to our unseen friends, Hal and Frank, in Los Angeles. Frank spoke to a doctor on the telephone, and we told all the details of the illness and what we had in our medical chest. In this way the doctor told us what to do.

We went to the boy and asked for a sharp knife and some boiling water. His mother became hysterical, and some of us had to keep the rest of the villagers away. All the hair was cut off the boy's head, the abscess was opened and cleaned, and we began the penicillin cure. Each evening we consulted the doctor in Los Angeles, and soon the boy's temperature fell, and he was laughing and wanting to look at pictures of the white man's strange world far away. A week later he was playing on the beach.

After this there was no end to the illness in the village: everyone wanted to consult us. When the medical chest was empty, we made cocoa and gave them that.

Some days later we were made citizens of Raroia and given Polynesian names. Tupuhoe led the ceremony and there was more singing and dancing.

One night we heard by wireless that the French Government had sent the schooner *Tamara* to fetch us to Tahiti, the only island near us which was in touch with the rest of the world. On another night later a vessel was reported lying at the entrance to the lagoon. We went to look and saw her lights. Was this the *Tamara*? Why did she not come in?

But then we saw that she was on an invisible coral reef. Torstein got a lamp and signalled to ask the name of the ship. The answer came back: "*Maoae*."

This was the regular schooner which came to the islands for copra. It was lucky that she lay in the shelter of the island and that the weather was quiet. But the current was treacherous.

Strong ropes were fastened to her and were rowed in to the land. Then the natives tied them to palms. Load after load of valuable copra was taken off and brought to land in canoes. But when day came the schooner was in a worse position on the reef than before. We could not pull her off, and if she stayed there she would be smashed to pieces on the reef.

Luckily, about noon the same day, the schooner *Tamara* arrived to fetch us, with important people on board. With some risk and a lot of skill, she pulled the *Maoae* off the reef into deep water; but water was pouring into her through holes and she had to be brought with all speed to the shallows in the lagoon. Then the best divers went down with lead plates and nails, and stopped up the worst holes so that she could be taken to Tahiti to be put right.

Our farewell to Raroia was more than sad. Everyone who could come was on the jetty. Tupuhoe was in the centre, holding the little boy by the hand. Both were crying; indeed there was not a dry eye on the jetty. The faithful people were losing six friends, and we were losing 127. We still remembered the strange music: ". . . and share memories with us so that we can always be together, even when you go away to a far land. Good day."

The *Tamara* towed the *Kon-Tiki* behind, and four days later we reached Tahiti. Its wild blue mountains rose to the sky, with clouds around the tops. On the sides of the mountains was the green vegetation of the South Seas, and in the valleys were the palms. All along the coast we could see a golden beach.

We sailed through an opening in the reef into the harbour of Papeete. Before us were the red roofs, half hidden by trees. Papeete is the capital of Tahiti, the only town in these islands. It is a city of pleasure, and the centre of government and trade.

The inhabitants stood waiting for us. The *pae-pae*

127

which had come from America was something everyone wanted to see. The *Kon-Tiki* was given a place of honour, and a little Polynesian girl presented us with an enormous wheel of Tahitian wild flowers. Other young girls hung sweet-smelling flowers round our necks as a welcome to Tahiti, the pearl of the South Seas.

We were received at the governor's palace and were invited to every corner of the friendly island. A great feast was given by the chief in his house in a valley, and we were given Tahitian names.

Those were carefree days under the sun and the drifting clouds. We bathed in the lagoon, climbed in the mountains, and danced the hula-hula on the grass under the palms. The days passed and became weeks. Then a message came from Norway saying that the ship *Thor I* had been ordered to proceed to Tahiti and take us to America.

Early one morning she arrived, and the *Kon-Tiki* was towed out to her and lifted on board. Brown and white people crowded round with farewell gifts and flowers.

"If you wish yourselves back at Tahiti," the chief cried, "you must throw a wreath into the lagoon when the boat goes."

The ropes were thrown off, the engines roared, and we moved away from Tahiti. Soon the red roofs disappeared behind the palms, and the palms themselves vanished in the blue mountains which sank like shadows into the Pacific.

Waves were breaking out on the blue sea, but we could no longer reach down to them. White clouds drifted across the blue sky. We were no longer travelling the same way. We were acting against Nature now. We were on our way to the twentieth century which lay so far, far away.

But the six of us on deck, standing beside our nine dear balsa logs, were grateful to be alive. And in the lagoon at Tahiti six white wreaths lay alone, washing in and out, in and out, with the little waves on the beach.

Dolphin

Flying fish

Squid

Crab

Pilot fish

Octopus

Frigate bird

Booby

Glossary

A

abscess: collection of bad liquid in one place in the body.

absorb: take in; suck in.

accurate: exact.

accursed: cursed.

A.D. (anno domini): after the birth of Christ.

aerial: wire, usually high up in the air, for collecting wireless signals.

Air Material Command: department which controls the material used by the Air Force.

aircraft: aeroplane or aeroplanes.

amateur: one who does a thing for pleasure and not for money.

ambassador: Minister sent by one country to represent it in a foreign country.

amid: in the middle of.

ancestor: man or woman of the past from whom the family is descended.

anchor: heavy mass of iron with a ring at one end for a rope and two pointed arms at the other; it is used for holding a ship and it is dropped into the sea.

antarctic: the coldest part of the world in the far south.

apparatus: scientific instrument.

architecture: science and planning of buildings.

artificially: in a way produced by art and not by nature.

ashore: on the shore.

asphalt: smooth, hard, black substance used for making roads and paths.

astern: at the back (of a ship).

athletic: powerful in body.

atoll: island made up of a ring of low rocks round a salt-water lake.

B

background: what can be seen at the back.

bait: food to attract fish.

balsa: kind of tree that grows in Peru; its wood is very light.

bamboo: stem of thick grass which grows in hot parts of the world.

bang: strike noisily.

barren: without plants.

battery: group of boxes from which an electric current may be got.

bloodstained: stained with blood.

booby: a kind of bird.

bow: front part of a ship.

breaker: heavy ocean wave which breaks.

bump: move while striking.

bungalow: house with only one floor.

133

bureau: office of a government department.
burnt-out: completely burnt and finished.

C

cabin: room on board a ship.
cactus: a kind of plant with sharp points and a thick stem.
calendar: system which fixes the beginning and length of the year, and its divisions.
canvas: coarse cloth, such as that used for sails.
capital: large amount of money such as that needed to start a business.
carefree: free from care.
cargo: goods which a ship carries.
carpet: covering for a floor.
carve: cut figures and other shapes in wood or stone.
centreboard: rather thin and long piece of wood pushed down between the logs of a raft.
chaos: complete disorder.
chart: map showing rocks and depths of the sea.
chew: crush between the teeth.
chink: narrow space.
chip: bit of wood split off larger piece.
chorus: music sung by several voices together.
clamber: climb with hands and feet.
clumsy: heavy and difficult to move.
cluster: bunch; group.
coca: Bolivian plant; when the leaves are chewed, they make people feel strong.
cocoa: powder made from seeds; it makes a hot, brown drink.
collision: violent meeting of moving objects.
comic: laughable.
compact: well joined together.
compass: instrument for finding the north, etc.
concussion: shock to the brain, caused by a violent blow.
consult: ask the advice of.
copra: dried centre part of the coconut.
coral: hard substance made by sea creatures and forming islands and rocks.
countless: very many.
crab: sea creature with eight legs and two pincers which walks sideways, forwards or backwards.
craft: ship; vessel.
crater: opening at the top of a volcano.
creak: sharp noise like that made by bending wood.
cross-current: current which moves across.
crystal: very clear glass; substance like this.

cuttle-fish: sea creature with ten arms; it sends out black liquid when it is trying to escape.

D

dazed: confused in mind.
delicious: very good to eat.
detect: discover the existence of.
develop: put a photographic film in liquids which make the pictures appear.
diary: daily record of events.
dinghy: kind of small boat.
disagreeable: unpleasant.
disaster: terrible event.
distracted: confused; having the attention drawn to other things.
dockyard: place where ships are built and repaired.
dolphin: fish famous for its change of colour when dying.
dressing-gown: long loose coat worn when dressing or when partly dressed.
due: exactly.

E

earphone: instrument placed over the ear, used by telephone and wireless operators.
east-north-east: half-way between east and north-east; $22\frac{1}{2}$ degrees north of east.
eddy: turning current.
eel: fish like a snake.
either: also (only after negatives).
eleventh hour: last moment.
embassy: house where the representative of a foreign country lives.
emphatically: with force in the words.
energetic: with energy.
enthusiasm: eagerness and pleasure.
entice: attract strongly.
entry: note written in a book.
equator: imaginary line round the earth passing through the hot countries and midway from north and south.
everyday: which happens every day; usual.
excellency: title placed before the names of Ministers, etc.

F

fathom: six feet.
fell: cause to fall; cut down.
film (v.): take moving pictures of.
financial: connected with money.

fire-arms: guns.

fist: closed hand.

fling: throw violently.

foam: white part of rough water.

foredeck: front part of the deck.

forefather: man of the past from whom the family is descended.

fortnight: two weeks.

founder: one who first started.

freshen: increase in strength.

frigate bird: large fast-flying bird found near land in the hot parts of the world.

fro: from (only in the phrase *to and fro*).

G

gale: rather strong wind.

gap: opening; empty space between.

generation: average time in which children are ready to take the place of parents (25–30 years).

genuine: real; not false.

gigantic: very big.

glider: flying machine like an aeroplane but without engines.

globe: earth.

goal: place one is trying to reach.

good deal: rather a lot; rather less than *great deal*.

great power: great and powerful country.

groove: long narrow hollow in the surface.

guarantee: promise certainly.

guitar: musical instrument with six strings played by the hand.

gust: sudden violent rush of wind.

H

half-breed: person of mixed blood.

harpoon: pointed rod with a rope fixed to the back for catching fish.

haul: pull strongly.

head towards: go towards.

heave: pull strongly.

helm: arrangement for steering.

helmsman: man who steers.

hemp: Indian plant used for making rope.

hew: cut with an axe.

hoist: raise; pull up.

horizon: line where sky and sea or land seem to meet.

hula-hula: south sea dance.

hysterical: having the nervous system distrubed: laughing madly.

I

ignorant: knowing little or nothing of.

immigrant: one who enters a country and settles in it.

imposing: important in appearance.

inclined plane: flat surface low at one end and rising steadily to the other.

incomprehensible: which cannot be understood.

incredibly: in a way difficult to believe.

indication: sign.

inevitable: which cannot be avoided.

inflate: fill with air.

infuriated: very angry.

ingenious: very clever.

inhabit: live in.

inspect: examine.

instructor: teacher.

intact: untouched; unbroken.

intelligent: quick to understand.

intensely: with deep feeling; violently.

invade: come into with force.

investigation: examination; inquiry.

investigator: one who examines a subject to discover the truth.

invisible: which cannot be seen.

involuntary: without intention.

islander: one who lives on an island.

isolated: separated from others; alone.

J

jaw: bone holding the teeth:

jeep: kind of small car much used in the army and for crossing rough ground.

jelly-fish: sea creature which stings; one can see through it.

jetty: long narrow thing built out from the land into the sea, at which ships and boats may land people and goods.

journalist: one who writes for the newspapers.

jungle: low, thickly growing forest.

jungle-clad: covered with jungle.

K

keel: the lowest piece of wood or metal of a ship or boat.
kettle: metal vessel for boiling water; it has a tube from which the water is poured.

L

lagoon: salt-water lake separated from the sea by a bank of sand or rock.
lash: tie firmly.
latitude: distance north or south measured in degrees.
lecture: speech on one subject for the purpose of teaching.
legend: story handed down from the past.
legendary: found in legends.
liana: kind of twisting plant in a tropical forest.
lifebelt: belt which floats well to support a body in water.
lifeboat: small boat carried by ships to save life if the ships sink.
line: rope.
log-book: book containing daily record of events on board.
longitude: distance, measured in degrees, east or west of a line through Greenwich near London.
lung: organ in the chest for breathing.
lush: thickly growing and full of juices.

M

manuscript: book written by hand and ready to be printed.
marine: connected with the sea and ships.
Marseillaise: French national song.
mast: upright to which a ship's sails are fixed.
masthead: top of the mast.
maximum: highest degree.
mesh: space between the threads of a net.
minimum: lowest degree.
minute: sixtieth part of a degree.
mirage: imaginary view produced in the air.
monolith: single block of stone.
monster: large and terrible creature.
monument: stone object put up for the purpose of making people remember.

N

naval: connected with warships.
navigate: direct the course of a ship.
navigator: one who can direct the course of a ship properly.
newcomer: one who has lately arrived.
northerly: of the north.
north-north-east: half-way between north and north-east; $22\frac{1}{2}$ degrees east of north.

O

obvious: very clear.
octopus: sea creature with eight arms coming from round the mouth.
on watch: watching.
operator: one who makes a machine or instrument work.
outpost: place (or group of men) at some distance in front of the rest.
outrigger: canoe which has a framework sticking out at the side to prevent it from turning over.
overboard: into the sea from a ship.
overwhelmed: overcome by one's feelings.

P

paddle: kind of oar with a blade at one end or each end; in use it is held in the hand and does not rest on the side of the boat.
palm: kind of tropical tree; some palms bear coconuts.
palm-clad: covered with palm trees.
paraffin: oil for lamps.
parallel: never meeting; always at the same distance from.
parrot: kind of bird with short hooked nose; it can be taught to speak.
penicillin: a substance which cures poisons in the body.
petrol: oil used for driving motor-cars.
pilot fish: small fish which swim in front of sharks.
pistol: small gun.
plank: long flat piece of smooth wood.
plankton: all the forms of floating creatures in the sea.
plantation: place where plants and trees are cultivated.
plug: stop up (a hole); fill up.
p.m.: after twelve o'clock noon.
postpone: arrange to hold at a later time.
prehistoric: belonging to the time before history began.
present (v.): introduce (one person to another).
prey: what is hunted and killed by an animal.
primitive: early and not yet developed.
pursue: follow after and try to catch.
pyramid: four-sided building with square base and pointed top.

Q

quarry: hole in the ground where stone is got.
quay: landing-place by the sea, or sticking out into the sea, for loading and unloading ships.
quench: stop (thirst).

R

racial : of the race.

radiant : smiling and very happy.

raft : flat floating vessel made of wood.

ration : fixed daily amount of food allowed to one person.

ray : fish with broad flat body rather like a shark.

reef : line of rock or sand about level with the surface of the sea.

refrigerate : make cold; freeze.

relationship : connection; degree of connection.

relax : loosen.

remove : take away.

roller : long swelling wave.

romance : feeling connected with imagination and adventure, happier than the feelings of ordinary life.

ruffian : rough person.

rust-red : brownish-red.

S

salute : greet; raise the hand to the head.

sap : juice of plants and trees.

saucer : curved plate used under a cup.

saunter : walk slowly.

schooner : sailing ship with two, three or four masts.

scrap : bit.

scrawl : write quickly and untidily.

seafarer : one who goes to sea; sailor.

sea-going : fit to go out to sea.

seaman : sailor.

sea-sick : ill as a result of the movement of a ship on the sea.

seaweed : plant which grows in the sea.

sensation : feeling.

sex : either of the two divisions of people distinguished as men and women.

sextant : instrument for measuring angles and finding one's position at sea.

shark : large and dangerous sea-fish.

shatter : break completely.

shrunken : having become smaller.

site : place for building.

skull : bones of the head.

slumber : sleep.

smack : hit with a flat surface.

smash: break badly.

sofa: long seat.

solitary: alone.

southernmost: farthest to the south.

specialist: person who studies a single part of a subject.

specialize: study one part of a subject very deeply.

spectrum: band of colours into which a beam of light may be divided after passing through glass of a certain shape.

speculate: think; wonder.

spike: sharp point.

splash: cause (liquid) to fly about.

spokesman: speaker who tells the ideas of all the group.

spurious: false.

squall: sudden violent storm of wind.

squid: kind of cuttle-fish.

stationary: not moving.

steamer: ship driven by steam.

steersman: man who steers.

stern: back part of a ship.

strand: run on land.

streak: irregular line or band (often with colours).

stubbornly: not yielding.

stumble: nearly fall while walking.

submerged: under the water.

supernatural: not natural; connected with spirits.

surf: foam of the sea breaking on shore or rocks.

survivor: one who is not killed in an accident.

T

tablet: small quantity of powder pressed together into one piece.

technical: connected with science, engineering or machines.

temporary: not fixed; lasting only a short time.

torch: lamp carried in the hand.

tow: pull.

trade-wind: unchanging wind which blows towards the equator from north-east and south-east.

transmitter: wireless instrument which sends out signals.

treacherous: not dependable; likely to fail in need.

triangle: figure with three straight sides.

triumphant: victorious.

tropical: connected with hot, damp parts of the world.

trough: low place between two waves.

tug: ship used for pulling others.

twinkle: shine with unsteady, dancing light.

U

ungovernable: which cannot be controlled.
utensil: vessel in common use in the house.

V

vague: not clear.
vegetation: plants.
vice-chief: man next in rank to the chief.
visible: which can be seen.
vocabulary: list of words.
volcano: mountain with an opening at the top through which hot and melted
    stones, and gases, are thrown up.

W

watch: man who watches on board ship.
week-end: free days at the end of the week (Saturday and Sunday).
west-north-west: half-way between west and north-west; 22½ degrees north of
    west.
whale: very large sea animal.
windward: in the direction from which the wind is blowing.
withered: dry and dead.
workshop: building in which work is done.
worn-out: completely tired.
wreath: circle of flowers.
wrinkled: line like that produced in the skin by old age.

Y

yacht: sailing ship used for pleasure.

THE BRIDGE SERIES

General Editor J A Bright